Just the Facts

INFORMATION MODELING
WITH BUSINESS COMMUNICATION

FIRST EDITION

Marco Wobben

Technics Publications
SEDONA, ARIZONA

115 Linda Vista
Sedona, AZ 86336 USA

https://www.TechnicsPub.com

Edited by Sadie Hoberman

Cover design by Lorena Molinari

All rights reserved. No part of this book may be reproduced or transmitted in any form or by any means, electronic or mechanical, including photocopying, recording or by any information storage and retrieval system, without written permission from the publisher, except for brief quotations in a review.

The authors and publisher have taken care in the preparation of this book but make no expressed or implied warranty of any kind and assume no responsibility for errors or omissions. No liability is assumed for incidental or consequential damages in connection with or arising out of the use of the information or programs contained herein.

All trade and product names are trademarks, registered trademarks, or service marks of their respective companies and are the property of their respective holders and should be treated as such.

First Printing 2024

Copyright © 2024 by Marco Wobben

ISBN, print ed.   9781634624336
ISBN, Kindle ed.   9781634624343
ISBN, PDF ed.   9781634624350

What can be said at all can be said clearly;
and whereof one cannot speak, thereof one must be silent.

Ludwig Wittgenstein

Contents

Acknowledgments _____ 1
Introduction _____ 3

Section One: Rationale _____ 5
1.   Business Information _____ 7
2.   Historical Overview _____ 13
   2.6 Management Challenge _____ 18
   2.7 Memes and Risks _____ 19
3.   Perspective on Communication _____ 21

Section Two: Business Employees and Domain Experts ____ 27
4.   Working with Facts _____ 29

Section Three: Business Information Modelers _____ 37
5.   Fact-oriented Modeling _____ 39
6.   Data Structures _____ 45
7.   Information Modeling _____ 51
   7.1.1 Collecting Facts _____ 52
   7.1.2 Sorting Facts _____ 53
   7.1.3 Analyzing Facts _____ 53
   7.1.5 Values _____ 54
   7.1.6 Objects _____ 54
   7.4.1 Non-atomic Facts _____ 59
   7.4.2 Non-concrete Facts _____ 59
   7.4.3 Non-unique Facts _____ 60
   7.4.4 Different Words, Same Facts _____ 60

8. Information Constraints _____ 65
8.6.1 Subtype _____ 73

9. Diagrams _____ 75

10. Information Model Elements _____ 87

Section Four: Data Modelers and Engineers _____ 101

11. Model Transformation _____ 103

12. Artifacts _____ 111

13. Appendix _____ 127
13.7.1 Transitional _____ 137
13.7.2 Temporal _____ 138
13.7.3 Multi-lingual _____ 139

References _____ 145
Books _____ 145
CaseTalk _____ 145
Methods _____ 147
Experts _____ 147

Index _____ 149

Figures

Figure 1: From data to wisdom. _____ 10
Figure 2: Graphical breakdown of a fact expression. _____ 33
Figure 3: Patient Source Records. _____ 45
Figure 4: Document Structure. _____ 46
Figure 5: NoSQL Structure. _____ 47
Figure 6: Logical structure. _____ 48
Figure 7: Graph structure. _____ 49
Figure 8: Patient Firstname grammar. _____ 56
Figure 9: Patient Checkup Day grammar. _____ 57
Figure 10: Employee Checkup grammar. _____ 57
Figure 11: Fact, grammar, and diagram. _____ 61
Figure 12: Dialog starting abstract and getting concrete. _____ 63
Figure 13: Inventory counts. _____ 63
Figure 14: Patient and checkup day identifiers. _____ 66
Figure 15: patient surname identify diagram. _____ 66
Figure 16: Facts comply to the N-1 rule. _____ 67
Figure 17: Graphical presentation of a mandatory constraint. _____ 68
Figure 18: Graphical representation of value constraints. _____ 70
Figure 19: Consistency across facts. _____ 71
Figure 20: Limiting the amount of facts. _____ 72
Figure 21: Employees can be a doctor or a nurse. _____ 73
Figure 22: FCO-IM diagram explained. _____ 76
Figure 23: Conceptual and logical data model. _____ 78
Figure 24: Physical data model. _____ 78
Figure 25: Logical data model with fact expressions. _____ 80
Figure 26: Database views to visualize object types. _____ 81
Figure 27: UML class diagram. _____ 82
Figure 28: UML class diagram with fact expressions. _____ 83
Figure 29: Concept map with fact expressions. _____ 84
Figure 30: Diagram with concepts and containers. _____ 88
Figure 31: Informal taxonomy. _____ 89
Figure 32: Formal taxonomy. _____ 90
Figure 33: Legal articles with references. _____ 93
Figure 34: Business rule description with references. _____ 96
Figure 35: Activity diagram with facts. _____ 98
Figure 36: Events involving various elements. _____ 99
Figure 37: Model transformation - Group. _____ 103

Figure 38: Model transformation - Lexicalize. _____ 104
Figure 39: Model transformation - Reduce. _____ 105
Figure 40: Lexicalizing to column store. _____ 106
Figure 41: Checkup Employee with a wide unicity constraint. _____ 107
Figure 42: Checkup Employee with a unicity constraint on checkup. _____ 107
Figure 43: Checkup Employee with a unicity constraint on Employee. ____ 107
Figure 44: Ensemble logical modeling artifact. _____ 108
Figure 45: Imported ensemble logical modeling artifact. _____ 109
Figure 46: Data Vault recognizes hubs, satellites, and links. _____ 109
Figure 47: Source system to information model mapping. _____ 113
Figure 48: Generated SQL DDL. _____ 115
Figure 49: Generated SQL DML. _____ 116
Figure 50: Generated SQL expression layer. _____ 116
Figure 51: Generated XSD snippet. _____ 118
Figure 52: Generated JSON snippet. _____ 119
Figure 53: Generated RDF/OWL snippet. _____ 121
Figure 54: Generated Python snippet. _____ 122
Figure 55: Generated spaCy snippet. _____ 123
Figure 56: Identical facts, different structure. _____ 128
Figure 57: Generalized objects can be multiple things. _____ 129
Figure 58: Recursive information structure. _____ 130
Figure 59: Support Request Information Model. _____ 131
Figure 60: Support Request UML Diagram. _____ 132
Figure 61: Decision table. _____ 133
Figure 62: Reduced decision table. _____ 133
Figure 63: Verbalized Decision Table. _____ 134
Figure 64: Modeled Decision Table. _____ 135
Figure 65: UML from decision table. _____ 136
Figure 66: Reference data and metadata modeling. _____ 137
Figure 67: Transitional fact. _____ 138
Figure 68: Temporal fact. _____ 139
Figure 69: Multi-lingual data. _____ 140
Figure 70: Multi lingual information model. _____ 140
Figure 71: CaseTalk screenprint. _____ 146

Acknowledgments

I would like to thank a few people, for I would not have written this book without them. First, the methods' founding fathers **Guido Bakema**, **JanPieter Zwart,** and **Harm van der Lek**. This would not have happened without them and the endless list of students, researchers, and developers who have worked with them.

Edward Langeland, for his thought-provoking discussions about the distinction between data and information, relentless questions about what I want to say in each paragraph, and bringing out-of-the-box ideas on how to present to stakeholders.

Ron Nagtegaal and Rob Arntz, who have used CaseTalk longer than anyone! Without their professional challenges and relentless requests for functionality and support, tools and theory would not be as practical today as they were when I started working with them.

George McGeachie, who printed an early draft to take with him on his vacation to provide me with feedback while simultaneously trying to understand my early writings and suggest improvements to make this a more pleasant experience for the reader.

Stephan Lorenz, for understanding the need for information models in a tech-heavy medical environment to build business-focused solutions. Thanks for providing insight through questions and business modeling needs.

My son, **Simon Wobben**, who kept asking for a copy of this book after he read that data is not information. He challenges his own teachers with questions about their data. He gives me hope for a future in a world where technology overwhelms everyone.

The love of my life, **Jody Johans**, who I met due to serendipity at the Data Modeling Zone in Portland in 2016, themed "Peace, Love, and Data Modeling." Needless to say, it changed both our lives hugely. In our almost daily talks about data, information, architecture, and cultural differences, she's my love, muse, and fellow nerd.

Introduction

This book is written for three distinct audiences, which should be working together seamlessly, but, in practice, do not seem to speak the same language. These audiences are the business side, the technical IT side, and the architects and modelers in the middle. This book is written to serve all three to give them insight, provide understanding, and achieve how to communicate as one.

For a general understanding, Section One explain the difference between data and information, provide a historical overview describing the many changes and modern-day challenges, and conclude which perspectives there are on communication.

The book then continues with sections intended for business employees, modelers, and engineers. You may read from start to finish, but you are also very welcome to dive straight into the section that interests you. Yet I do hope you'll read all of them in time. To effectively communicate with counterparts in the organization, understand where they are from, along with their challenges and needs.

SECTION ONE

Rationale

For all readers to understand there is a difference between data and information, and we did not invent it all on the spot, some knowledge of history is required. And if we do not understand where we come from, we might not understand where we are or where we are going. And for those who do not know history are bound to repeat themselves.

In this section, we provide the overview that lays out the sections after that. You may read it regardless of your interest or role in the organization. It'll hopefully create a common understanding and the need to communicate together.

The general overview runs from Chapters 1 to 3.

1. Business Information

Welcome to the intriguing realm where data seems to be everywhere we look. It runs in apps and drives businesses, requires tons of technology, and shapes public opinions and politics. As data affects our daily lives and separates people into different groups, we should be paying more attention to what the data is about and how we communicate as human beings.

It is not the data itself but our communication about the data that builds bridges of understanding. This book aims to bring a holistic view to three distinctive audiences, enabling all to communicate about data, share information, and communicate more effectively, aligning goals and collaborating seamlessly. Thanks to our human capability to communicate, we can build bridges that connect people, transcend silos, and align technology in a way that propels organizations forward into this digital age.

Whether you are a business visionary, a tech enthusiast, or someone navigating the ever-changing landscape of data, this book is your roadmap to a future where communication, technology, and business harmoniously coexist. As you embark on this journey, you'll find that the book caters to three audiences:

- **Business Employees and Domain Experts.** The first and second sections brings business into focus. We address the needs of business employees and domain experts who are at the forefront of operations and strategy. We explore how they can harness the power of communication to contribute to the success of the organization.

- **Business Information Modelers**. The third section delves into the realm of information modeling. Here, we cater to the audience whose expertise lies in capturing and documenting business information and ensure it lays out the guidelines to help IT provide products and services that meet the business needs and requirements.

- **Developers and Engineers**. The fourth section focuses on the data modelers and engineers who form the backbone of technology implementation. It dives deeper into the intricate world of data, and transforming raw data into valuable information, insights, applications, databases, and AI.

1.1 Communication

In collaborative environments, individuals share information about their experiences. Human history began with the oral transmission of facts, progressed with the advent of the printing press, and has now reached a digital era where computers can store and process this information. Despite these advancements, the fundamental purpose of communication remains unchanged: the dissemination of information.

The use of natural language is indispensable for integrating communication, metadata and data. Natural language, the spoken language of people, enables us to convey not only data but also its significance and the context surrounding it.

1.2 Data versus Information

The word "data" has an interesting linguistic history. It originates from the Latin word "datum," the singular form of "data," which means "something given" or "a fact." In the context of information, "data" refers to individual facts, statistics, or pieces of information, often in raw or unprocessed form.

In current times, "data" typically refers to discrete pieces of information that can be collected, stored, and processed electronically. Data can take various forms, including numbers, text, images, or multimedia, and provides the foundation for meaningful information through analysis and interpretation.

On the other hand, "information" refers to organized, processed, and contextualized data, that is meaningful and useful. Information answers questions, provides insights, and facilitates decision-making. The subtle, yet crucial difference between "data" and "information" is illustrated in the following example:

- **Data**: Imagine a series of numbers, like "1, 2, 3, 4, 5." These are data points. They are like puzzle pieces, separate and unprocessed.

- **Information**: Now, imagine you're told that these numbers represent the sequence of the first five natural numbers. This context and structure make these numbers meaningful and useful, becoming information.

As another example of the importance of context, we see a list of names: Sydney, Houston, Amsterdam. This data can represent a list of cities or named meeting rooms at a venue. This data is synonymous with information only to those familiar with the correct context.

An even more extended list is the following, where the bits and bytes are stored in small units called tokens. We can recognize the data by adding syntax to these bits and bytes. Given the context we arrive at information, the meaning brings us knowledge to finally arrive at the required wisdom to go to the store to buy cookies and milk.

```
Token:          20221222
Data:           Date 22-12-2022
Information:    22-12-2022 is a winter day
Knowledge:      Almost Christmas
Wisdom:         Buy cookies and milk for Santa
```

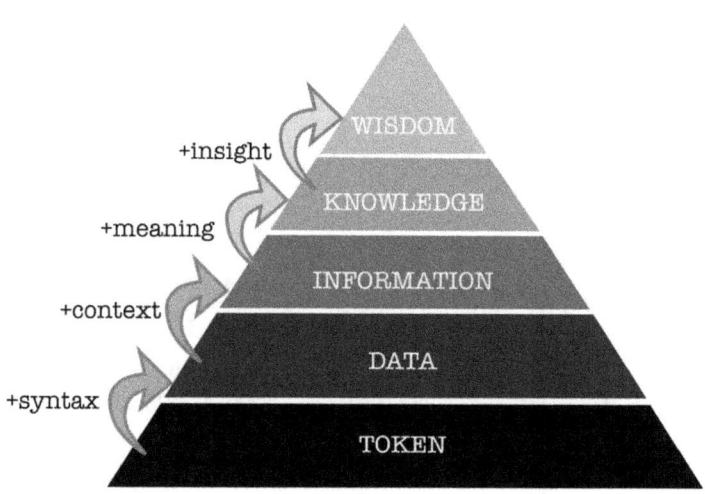

Figure 1: From data to wisdom.

Although this pyramid makes perfect sense, it also shows the effort involved before anyone can truly make sense of our data. The good news is that IT products mostly hide tokens, and we can start with data instead. The bad news is that our data has been almost entirely stripped of insights, meaning, and context.

But let's not despair. This book provides one way of capturing business information without stripping it down to just data. But remember, it is more about understanding, documenting, and modeling the information than just about the data. Usually, when things go wrong when it comes to data, the first question is, "What does that mean?" and that can only be answered if we truly understand it in the first place.

Before you continue reading, it might be important to note it's not just about the data, data model, or information model perse. The act of modeling serves to communicate the needs of the organization. The act of information modeling allows us all to engage with each other, using a method to align our communication and document this alignment simultaneously to develop a shared understanding without diving into the technical aspects of data automation.

2. Historical Overview

Before delving further into the book, let's take a moment to reflect on the historical journey that has led us to our present-day complex landscape of hardware, software, data, and information. It's essential to see a glimpse of the complexity, the progress we've made, the challenges we've encountered, and the pressing need for robust methodologies for handling information as we navigate into the future.

---

*"Those who cannot remember the past
are condemned to repeat it."*

George Santayana

The evolution of information has been marked by a series of significant transformations over time, reflecting the changing needs and complexities of our modern world. From speech and Stone Age paintings to writings on paper and the mechanical printing press, from computed calculations to large-scale digital sharing of information, we find ourselves in a fast-growing era of digitized information. IT is decades in development, yet young when it comes to accurately managing business information, meaning, and context across the business-IT boundaries. To better understand some of that complexity, let's list some developments.

2.1 People

- **Digital sharing:** We transitioned from manual (vocal) to mechanical (printing) to digital sharing of information (computers). The digital era brought along new specialists who are required to convert the knowledge of domain experts for digital use and sharing.

- **Scaling of Expertise:** The increasing scale of automation led to a proliferation of new roles: business analysts, functional designers, technical designers, developers, architects, and specialized management. Even the experts needed more expertise, and we found ourselves needing front-end developers, back-end developers, data modelers, process modelers, solution architects, software architects, enterprise architects, data architects, information architects, and many more roles.

2.2 Systems

- **Hardware Evolution:** The shift from mainframes to personal computers to mobile devices and websites resulted in a plethora of isolated workspaces, each with its distinct data storage and system requirements, each functioning as separate silos.

- **Web and Mobile Applications:** The fast pace of website and mobile app development adds to the complexity. With software and data platforms getting developed faster to respond to a changing market and business needs, the focus on integrating data has been lost in favor of fast software development and delivery.

2.3 Data

- **Relational Databases:** Technology evolved from paper to tape, via computer files to relational databases, allowing for optimized and consistent data storage and handling across multiple users of an application. Beyond relational databases, we now have unstructured data, document structures, virtual data, cloud storage, and many more solutions.

- **Data Warehousing, Lakes, and Meshes:** Data warehousing technologies emerged to integrate multiple databases to overcome issues caused by disconnected databases and a lack of historicization. The greatest advantage was integrating structured data from various applications while preserving historical data. Harmonizing this has been and continues to be a problem. It is a hard battle to unify the data in a way the business recognizes its information. Pouring data streams from devices, unstructured documents, and event logs, into the mix and building data lakes and data-mesh does not diminish the challenges.

- **Challenges in Integration:** In contrast to the long-standing traditions of accounting and finance, the enterprise landscape is now marked by countless technological challenges in integrating data to provide meaningful business information. All data products are an aftermath of the problem created over decades, and integrating them at a technical data level is sometimes a near-impossible challenge.

2.4 Software

- **Development Platforms:** The evolution of development platforms ranges from machine code to higher programming languages, from model-based 4GLs to individual users managing data in Excel worksheets and MS-Access files. The diverse environments all handle data differently, making it harder to unify.

- **Microservices and Fragmentation:** The introduction of web- and microservices were aimed at decoupling software components in favor of stable data delivery and reuse. This technological fragmentation of data continues into data contracts, data events, data pipelines, big data, and data mesh.

- **Agile Methodology:** The software development methodology shifted from long-running development cycles, called waterfall, to an Agile approach with smaller value and increasing cycles. In practice, too often, quick delivery is prioritized over comprehensive design and proper data integrations, and in some cases, it becomes the new dogma.

- **Data Governance and AI:** As governments introduce regulations like GDPR to protect the data of individuals, companies face a pressing need for data governance. And the advent of AI relies on accurate, factually correct, and verified data, making proper governance and meaningful information essential.

2.5 Business Information Challenge

As we've seen, data was designed and employed in relative isolation. Applications were crafted to address specific, often limited, business domains or processes, leaving data to exist in separate silos and be contextually rich. However, data has become ubiquitous. It permeates every facet of our digital existence, from personal interactions to complex business operations. As a result, coordination has emerged as imperative, both from a management and a technical standpoint.

Business knowledge has evolved into a strategic resource. It's no longer sufficient to merely collect and store data; organizations must meticulously orchestrate and govern the flow of data to be rich in context before it can become meaningful and useful information. This entails understanding the sources, ensuring its quality, managing its lifecycle, and safeguarding its security and privacy. It requires a holistic and proactive approach that aligns 'data'-management with business objectives.

On the technical front, the coordination of data is equally pivotal. With data often residing in various systems, platforms, and formats, there is a pressing need for seamless integration. The ability to exchange, transform, and analyze data across diverse environments has become the linchpin of modern digital operations. It demands flexible architectures and robust models, and technology-agnostic information models. So, where do we stand today, and what lies ahead? In our interconnected, data-driven world, the road forward demands a combination of technical prowess, methodological discipline, and a deep understanding of the evolving data landscape. It calls for adopting information management to ensure that data is not just a resource but a strategic asset that powers innovation, informs decisions, and facilitates collaboration. The challenges and opportunities are abundant. Our collective endeavor is to bring focus to this landscape with agility, purpose, and a commitment to harnessing the full potential of business information in the digital age.

2.6 Management Challenge

Many, if not all systems, are simply about storing, retrieving, or moving data. Data specialists handle the distribution of data from source to target, often being or working with developers, data engineers, business intelligence specialists, and data scientists. Ensuring meticulous tracking of data usage and users and providing the technology to facilitate this process accurately all fall within the purview of the horizontal architecture.

In the realm of governance, government, management, politics, and boardroom meetings, guidelines and legal articles outlining acceptable behaviors dictate what to adhere to and what to avoid. These directives rarely delve into the intricate details of handling the needed information, even as we continue to develop increasingly data-centric systems.

To effectively manage this so-called vertical architecture, which traces the requirements from the top-level management to the very implementation of systems and storage of data, it's crucial to establish a seamless connection between guidelines and requirements, as well as the data they pertain to. This architecture allows for the efficient tracking of policy changes and their implications on the systems we must adapt to reflect these modifications. Moreover, it provides a mechanism for demonstrating the policies under which we store data, ensuring accountability, see also 10.4 on Paragraphs.

2.7 Memes and Risks

The data life cycle concept prompts a significant question: Is data primarily shaped by the business's activities or a byproduct of software? In today's modern landscape, the relationship between business and data has become so deeply intertwined that the lines of distinction often blur. In some organizations, information technology (IT) drives the business, while in others, IT seamlessly integrates into the core of the business, sometimes without full recognition of this transformation.

Genuine ownership of data is increasingly vital, and addressing its life cycle across the horizontal architecture is essential to preserve data quality and, in turn, the information it conveys. To achieve a comprehensive understanding of the life cycle, it's crucial to record the *how, what, who, why, when, and where* in information. This information ensures that stored data remains useful for future analysis and utilization.

Data bias, a pervasive issue in data-driven decision-making, often arises from the uneven representation of certain groups or attributes in datasets. It can result from historical inequalities, data collection methods, or even the absence of critical data points. However, it's essential to recognize that not only the presence of bias but also the absence of data can create unknown or even unseen bias. When critical data is missing or underrepresented, it can lead to skewed perceptions and conclusions.

Decision-makers may, therefore, unknowingly rely on incomplete, false, or one-sided information, perpetuating existing biases or overlooking crucial insights. To address bias effectively, it's crucial to not only mitigate existing bias but also fill data gaps and ensure comprehensive, representative datasets, fostering more equitable and informed decision-making.

These problems are not easily solved by viewing things as a data problem. They are an information problem. Technology is helpful, but never enough. Understanding data in the correct context is crucial in providing correct information.

With all the challenges of scaling, integration, and emergence of new data technologies, the necessity for an enterprise-level information model to coordinate all our needs should be evident by now. We have a far better chance of doing things correctly if we can seamlessly integrate the known context with data, and the domain experts are involved to verify its correctness.

WISDOM FROM THE MEME MACHINE.

3. Perspective on Communication

Effective communication and consistent semantics are essential in both business and IT to avoid misunderstandings, errors, and inefficiencies. Clear definitions, common understanding, and structured information enable organizations to make better decisions, improve processes, and drive innovation. Knowing the context of data to understand what it means to the business allows IT professionals to provide real business value and service. Simultaneously, it allows all stakeholders to develop a shared language to improve communication. So, whether you're a business professional or an IT specialist, recognizing the importance of context and semantics in handling data to form information is key to success for the entire organization.

Both business and IT experts are equally important when dealing with data and information. Let's explore their roles in each context:

3.1 From a Business Perspective

- **Effective Communication:** In business, clear and effective communication is crucial. For businesses to communicate their strategies, goals, and performance to various stakeholders, such as employees, customers, investors, and partners, accurate and well-structured information is essential for making good decisions and conveying messages with precision.

- **Semantic Clarity**: Business terminology and semantics must be consistent to avoid confusion and misinterpretation. Inconsistent or ambiguous use of terms can lead to misunderstandings and inefficiencies. Establishing a shared vocabulary and ensuring that everyone understands and uses the same definitions is vital.

- **Decision-Making**: Businesses use data to support decision-making. Before that data is useful, semantic clarity is required to become information. That helps executives and managers draw accurate conclusions and develop strategies based on trustworthy information.

3.2 From an IT Perspective

- **Data Modeling**: IT professionals use data models to represent data and its relationships. The traditional purpose of data modeling is to describe the structure of data as understood and needed by the business for optimal handling and storage of that data. Yet, with the ever-increasing amount of technology, this no longer suffices to serve all requirements for system design. Information models provide a structured way to define the meaning of business knowledge while keeping technology at arm's length. We can use rich information models to generate data models and other technical notations without compromising the business information.

- **Metadata Management**: Metadata is strictly speaking data about data, that provides some context for data and is an essential part of IT systems. Clear and standardized metadata ensures data can be effectively located, understood, and managed. Relating the metadata to business information and definitions is paramount in an increasing world of technologies and an increasing lack of cohesion and coherence across the enterprise. Metadata ranges from describing types of data, to ownerships, departments, comments, and so on. Metadata is not a model that describes functions or processes. There are other types of models serving different needs. Business processes or functions do operate on data but are not metadata itself.

- **Data Integration**: In IT, it is critical to ensure that data from various sources can be integrated and understood. Data may come in different formats and structures, and consistent semantics are necessary for consistent and accurate integration. Semantic interoperability, where systems can understand and process data from various sources, is a key concern. Semantic interoperability is needed for the business to verify its correctness.

- **Data Governance**: Data governance frameworks ensure data quality, security, and compliance. The need for data governance is best steered by knowing the information it beholds and represents. Hence, data governance can be perceived as a technical requirement, whereas it is far more of a business requirement. The quality, security, and compliance needs are easier to understand when viewed as quality of information, security of information, and information compliance, instead of just the data.

3.3 Perspectives from Fact-oriented Modeling

The business need for facts is not new, nor surprising. The roots can be traced to research into semantic modeling for information systems in Europe during the 1970s. There were many pioneers, and this summary does not mention them all. An early contribution came in 1973 when Michael Senko wrote about "data structuring" in the IBM Systems Journal. In 1974, Jean-Raymond Abrial contributed an article on "Data Semantics." In June 1975, Eckhard Falkenberg's doctoral thesis was published, and in 1976, one of Falkenberg's papers mentions the term "object-role model".

- **NIAM** G.M. Nijssen made fundamental contributions by introducing the "circle-box" notation for object types and roles and formulating the first version of the conceptual schema design procedure. Robert Meersman extended the approach by adding subtyping and introducing the first truly conceptual query language. In the mid-1970s, his research team at the Control Data Corporation Research Laboratory in Belgium, and later at the University of Queensland, Australia, in the 1980s, developed the "Natural language Information Analysis Methodology."

- **ORM** In 1989, Terry Halpin completed his Ph.D. thesis on ORM, providing the first full formalization of the approach and incorporating several extensions. Also in 1989, Terry Halpin and G.M. Nijssen co-authored the book "Conceptual Schema and Relational Database Design" and several joint papers, providing the first formalization of object–role modeling.

- **FCO-IM** Also evolving from NIAM is *Fully Communication Oriented Information Modeling* (FCO-IM), created by Bakema, Zwart and Van Der Lek in 1992. It distinguishes itself from traditional ORM by taking a strict communication-oriented perspective. Rather than attempting to model the domain and its essential concepts, it models the communication in this domain (universe of discourse). Another important difference is that it does this on the level of concrete examples to find object-, fact-, and value types.

- **CaseTalk** (2002, BCP Software) is the commercial continuation of tool development to support the FCO-IM method. With the retirement of research staff (2010), BCP Software took the lead in theoretical research as part of new tool development. CaseTalk extended FCO-IM with numerous new functionalities over the years. It now supports multi-user, multi-version, and multi-lingual modeling; on-the-fly model-to-model transformations to conceptual, logical, and physical data models; export and generate to UML artifacts; source code generators, and data models in PowerDesigner, ER/Studio, and specifications for Data Vault Builder, and much more.

Tool support is crucial for any theory to stay alive. CaseTalk provides that lifeline for FCO-IM while providing invaluable information modeling functionality to a wide audience. This book contains many diagrams created in CaseTalk (see References, page 145).

SECTION TWO

Business Employees and Domain Experts

In this section, we bring business into sharp focus. We address the needs of business employees and domain experts, who are at the forefront of operations and strategy. We explore how to harness the power of communication to contribute to the success of the organization.

4. Working with Facts

The simplest and most fundamental way of using language to communicate is through stating facts. Facts contain the natural language and the concrete data values being conveyed. By expressing data in the form of facts, we make it easier to comprehend and work with the information. Facts serve as the contextual rich building blocks for effective communication and understanding within an organization.

> **Fact**: A thing that is known or proved to be true; Information used as evidence or as part of a report or news article; The truth about events as opposed to interpretation.

4.1 Business Domains

An information model focuses on describing the structure of information. Each information model is naturally limited to a specific subject or domain, known as the Universe of Discourse. It encompasses the communication bound within this area. The information model adheres to formal rules governing the information structure, validity, and usage.

To support the information flow effectively and accurately within an organization through automation, it is crucial to have a precise overview of the information needed. This is where an information model comes into play. It acts as a map, encompassing all information communicated between individuals, individuals and machines, and machines themselves. It encompasses not only individual information elements and their relations. The information model serves as a dictionary, giving terms and concepts meaning. And even more importantly, it reflects the perspective of the organization's business employees and domain experts, rather than being led by ever-changing technology.

A well-developed information model within an organization ensures the alignment of relevant concepts and definitions, leading to improved communication and collaboration among stakeholders. It serves as the foundation for information management across departments, applications, and data sources.

For instance, a robust information model plays a crucial role in communicating with external entities, emphasizing concepts such as liability, reliability, and accuracy. Due to its close connection to business operations, the information model becomes an excellent basis for automation. It serves as the specification for implementing the systems, ensuring precise alignment with the organization's communication and information needs. Consistency in terminology and information definitions is paramount for successfully automating systems.

4.2 Domain Expert

Information modeling requires skill, yet it is not a technical skill or an isolated engineering task. Information analysts collaborate with domain experts who possess the real expertise in the subject, to capture their knowledge and help them develop clear communication.

Domain experts play a crucial role in providing the necessary input for the information model. They provide concrete examples of information relevant to the domain. Additionally, domain experts play a vital role in verifying the outcomes of each modeling activity. They assess whether the fact statements accurately express the information, and ensure that the resulting phrases represent recognizable concepts and adhere to the correct business rules.

Different domain experts may have varying perspectives, opinions, and interpretations regarding what is important, the meaning of specific terms, and the applicable business rules. As a result, information analysts must navigate these differences of opinion, negotiate, make compromises, define boundaries, and assist in resolving conflicts in communication.

This highlights that information modeling is not solely a technical activity but also a social process. As information analysts, it is crucial to remember this during our daily work because work can get politically charged.

In the end, the information model (and the related generated artifacts) seems the most tangible product of the modeling process. However, in this information modeling process, we often resolve many assumptions, misunderstandings, and ambiguities that would otherwise not have been detected or addressed. In addition to improving the end results, the model also improves the understanding and communication of the domain experts.

4.3 Natural Language

In the realm of modeling, using abstract terms leads to ambiguity and uncertainty. The truth of any statement may not be clear unless we have well-defined definitions and context. For instance, consider the following expression:

```
"The flight takes eight hours."
```

Without further context, it is difficult to determine what is meant by "the flight" and how the duration is measured. Is it referring to an escape, a plane, or a bird in the sky? To establish clarity and ensure a shared understanding, we must provide the proper context and our statements require concrete examples. For example, we can specify:

```
"Flight KL886 departing from airport AMS at 2019/01/01 13:51h,
    takes 8 hours to arrive at the destination."
```

This fact, which contains concrete examples, allows us to verify the meaning and usage of terms by providing tangible context.

The distinction between double quotes and single quotes in language also plays a significant role in information modeling.

Fact expressions are always enclosed in double quotes. Using single quotes, we can enclose a phrasing inside the expression. For example:

```
"'John Smith' lives in 'The Netherlands'."
```

In this fact expression, we speak of a city residence containing references to citizen 'John Smith', and the country 'The Netherlands.' These are not just data values but refer to concepts bearing meaning. The use of single quotes in language refers to other things or concepts. In information modeling, the double quotes facts are called fact expressions. The phrases inside it, referring to other concepts or objects, are called Object Expressions. More on this topic will be explained in Chapter 5 and onwards (Section Three).

Using the approach of information modeling allows domain experts to speak in their own natural language. The method is well-equipped to support the discovery of Objects (things) and Labels (values) in the language of the domain experts. The language, the structure, and the values are part of the information model. The model documents every discovery in detail and, as we will see, is the building block for system development and business information.

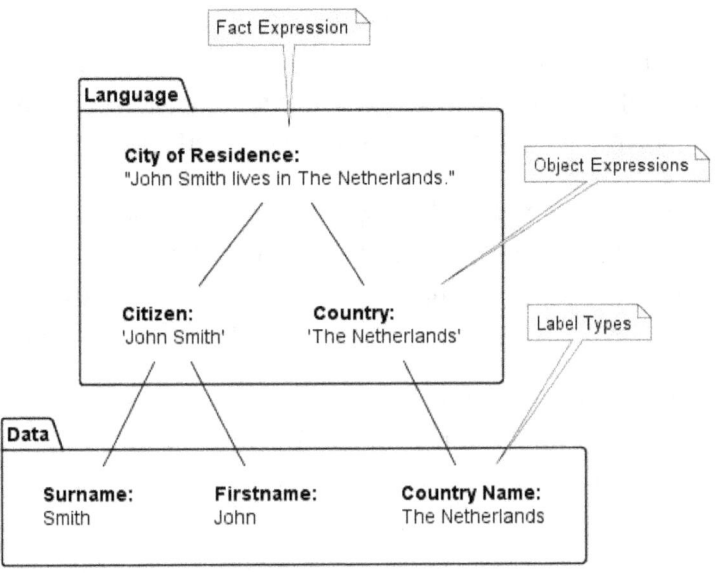

Figure 2: Graphical breakdown of a fact expression.

4.4 Fact-Oriented Modeling Benefits

Fact-oriented modeling offers advantages that make it an invaluable asset for businesses seeking to optimize their data management and information systems. Here are some of the key reasons your organization should care about information modeling using facts:

- **Clear and Unambiguous Understanding**: Fact-oriented modeling excels in capturing the essence of the business domain by focusing on facts, which are indisputable pieces of information. This clarity and precision help all stakeholders understand the model, reducing misunderstandings and misinterpretations.

- **Intense User Participation**: Fact-oriented modeling encourages active involvement from business users and domain experts. This direct engagement ensures that the model is aligned with the business's needs and requirements, enhancing its accuracy and relevance.

- **Enhanced Data Quality**: By emphasizing the semantics of data and ensuring that it accurately represents the business domain, fact-oriented modeling contributes to higher data quality. This, in turn, leads to more reliable and trustworthy information for decision-making.

- **Support for Agile Development**: Fact-oriented modeling allows businesses to extend the model fact by fact, making it well-suited for Agile methodologies. This flexibility enables rapid adjustments and improvements as business needs evolve.

- **Natural Language Documentation**: The use of natural language in fact-oriented modeling results in clear and comprehensible documentation of business semantics. This documentation is accessible to non-experts, ensuring that everyone involved can understand the model.

- **Seamless Validation**: Fact-oriented models are designed for easy validation by business users, regardless of their modeling expertise. This empowers users to actively participate in the verification process, promoting the accuracy and relevance of the information model.

- **Effective Model Transformations**: Fact-oriented modeling facilitates smooth model-to-model transformations while preserving the language of the business. This means that changes and adaptations in the model can be carried out efficiently without losing sight of the business's context and needs.

- **Reduction of Data Bias**: Fact-oriented modeling encourages a systematic approach to data representation, reducing the risk of data bias or incorrect assumptions. This is especially important in today's data-driven decision-making environment.

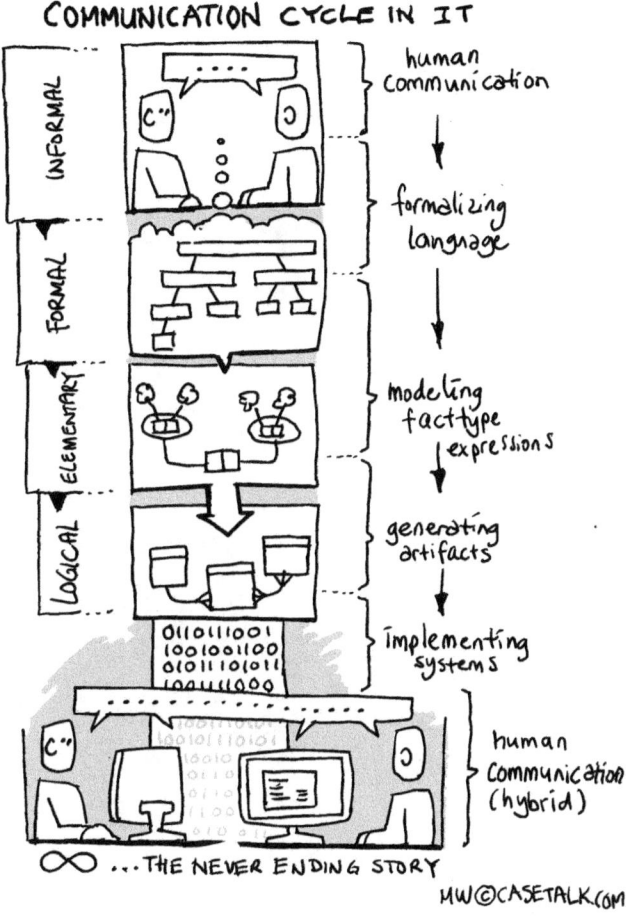

Incorporating fact-oriented modeling into data practices is an investment in the clarity, accuracy, and adaptability of your data and information systems. It empowers businesses to make well-informed decisions, enhances collaboration between business and IT, and ensures that data truly serves as an asset, driving success and innovation.

SECTION THREE

Business Information Modelers

In this section, we delve into the realm of information modeling itself. Here, we cater to the audience whose expertise lies in documenting the meaning, definitions, and relationships in business information. We uncover the art and science of building robust information structures.

5. Fact-oriented Modeling

Models represent the workings and needs of an organization and facilitate communication amongst colleagues and disciplines in any organization. The process of modeling is a craft that demands many years of experience combined with business domain experts. Through exploring sources and interviewing experts, diagrams are drawn up based on the knowledge gathered.

The drawings of boxes, lines, and arrows are a representation of the business knowledge as understood by the modeler. Many business experts will have a hard time verifying what is drawn up. Graphical symbols hide assumptions that are non-sensical to non-modelers. When models become larger, as more business knowledge is added, even skilled modelers will have a hard time fully understanding the meaning. It simply lacks consistent descriptions of how it is supposed to be used and what it means to the business. And there are no methods to reliably verify those diagrams or have them verified by business experts. Additional documentation is required to explain the meaning, use, and context. For models to be effective and of a high quality, they require documenting the communication from start to finish.

This is where fact-oriented information modeling excels. Fact-oriented modeling theory has been in development since the seventies and before, on different continents worldwide. With a strong focus on the business side of the information, these methods make that knowledge accessible to both knowledgeable and non-knowledgeable people alike.

Modelers dealing with complex business information can benefit greatly from adopting the fact-oriented approach, as it provides tools to help during interviews, limits the number of assumptions, and clarifies the complexity of the business knowledge. Similarly, businesses with a large quantity of data types can benefit from this approach for it documents and validates all details, no matter how large the models become.

5.1 Fully Communication Oriented Information Modeling

FCO-IM is a continuation in the early nineties by three Dutchmen: Guido Bakema, JanPieter Zwart, and Harm van der Lek. Through their roles as professors, teachers, and consultants, and their unwavering dedication, this method has matured over time, gained widespread recognition in schools and universities, and has proven its value in both small and large enterprises.

In this chapter, we describe the core principles and techniques of FCO-IM. It explores its applications and unique capabilities in bridging the gap between business language and technological implementations. By understanding the nuances of FCO-IM, you will be equipped with the knowledge to navigate the complexities of business information modeling.

Before proceeding further, there are a few prerequisites to remember. Throughout the book, we will break down the content into digestible steps, allowing you to skip sections you are already familiar with or revisit concepts you may have missed. Additionally, we use diagrams from the FCO-IM tool called CaseTalk. However, keep in mind that mastery of FCO-IM requires practice. While communicating in concrete facts may initially pose challenges for some, the benefits gained from tackling this approach will be tremendous, as listed in the next paragraph. References to dive deeper into the method appear in the back of this book.

5.2 Pros of FCO-IM

Chances are, you've seen or are already familiar with models that focus on tables with columns and foreign keys, and entities or classes with properties and relationships. These models are mostly graphic-based and drawn by hand to visualize and understand businesses from a data-centric perspective.

Those modeling approaches are an abstraction of the perceived business world and have data structures in mind. These models lack the ability to capture how business experts communicate about their data in the requirements-gathering phases. These abstract and sometimes technical models are hard for business experts or colleagues to verify without any form of documentation explaining how they reflect the business information.

Where domain experts usually lack the capability to communicate in technical models, the professionals who build those models often lack the ability to communicate in business language. There's a Tower of Babel effect in play here that cannot be overcome unless everyone starts sharing the same language, the language of the domain experts themselves.

> *In contrast, FCO-IM takes the approach of capturing how domain experts and business users communicate about their data in their own natural language. It is their communication that truly reflects the information in its proper context, in a readable and verifiable form. This process is very different from the modelers' invisible mental process of drawing diagrams.*

By adopting FCO-IM, everyone in the organization can participate in the communication and capture it to specify and/or verify each step of the modeling process. The main traits that make FCO-IM better than other modeling techniques are:

Non-technical: FCO-IM focuses on the aspects of meaning and its context rather than the technical details of automation, making it accessible to a wider audience and making it easier to serve a wide variety of technologies. This makes it a truly conceptual approach.

Precise and unambiguous: FCO-IM emphasizes accuracy, ensuring the information model is precise and leaves no room for ambiguity. It handles synonyms and homonyms with very little difficulty or lists potential issues we must tackle by clearing up business miscommunication. Anything that cannot be stated clearly requires more investigation and is helping the overall quality of the information model.

Not abstract: FCO-IM deals with real examples and concrete scenarios, making it practical and applicable to real-world situations. Almost all miscommunications arising from abstraction can be neutralized by providing an example to illustrate what is truly meant. This has a grounding effect in interviews that would otherwise remain abstract and ambiguous.

Natural language: FCO-IM utilizes natural language, enabling business stakeholders to understand and actively participate in the modeling process. It enables all in the organization to read in their own language how experts talk amongst each other and manage data.

5.3 The approach

Fact-oriented modeling involves the following series of activities that form a step-wise approach to make the information modeling process transparent and consistent:

- **Collecting**: Gathering relevant sources and documents, conducting interviews with domain experts, studying existing IT systems, and reading reports to obtain the necessary material for documenting facts. Facts serve as the building blocks of our information models.

- **Sorting:** The sorting process begins once facts have been documented. Facts are grouped and named according to their type.

- **Analyzing**: We find object and value types by analyzing the gathered facts. The analysis step includes adding constraints to the object and value types and relationships to ensure consistency of handling data.

- **Validating**: Domain experts must review and validate the information models using reports that include verbalized rules and expressions in natural language. Fact-oriented modeling is a cyclic process that involves continuous feedback and refinement of the model, making it an iterative and agile approach. Also, a product like CaseTalk validates the model for technical correctness and consistency to help the modelers themselves.

- **Generating:** By following the steps above and incorporating validation and feedback loops, fact-oriented information modeling continually improves the value and accuracy of the information model. To cross the bridge towards technology, CaseTalk transforms the information model into a various set of artifacts for our technical staff as described in the paragraph, Model Transformations (Section Four).

6. Data Structures

In information modeling, the process of verbalizing facts plays a crucial role in capturing and organizing meaningful elements of communication within an organization. Let's consider some simplified reports found in a small medical practice where blood pressure measurements are recorded during visits, called checkups. Imagine how the data can be structured, stored, and managed by the application to support the administrative tasks of the domain experts.

Patient number:	564432
Patient name:	Tom Harvey
Birth date:	1963/12/25
Gender:	male / ~~female~~

Date	Systolic	Diastolic
2010/10/13	170	110
2011/10/12	160	105
2012/10/24	160	95

Patient number:	587669
Patient name:	Leonard Reed
Birth date:	1955/07/13
Gender:	male / ~~female~~

Date	Systolic	Diastolic
2011/09/09	150	100
2012/09/24	150	95

Figure 3: Patient Source Records.

6.1 Document Structures

Documents contain relevant and related information in a single file. Similarly, the technical document-based structures follow that same paradigm. They are using hierarchical formats such as XML or JSON. They start with a root element which contains detail elements, which can contain more details again, etc. Visually, Figure 4 can be presented in a document structure.

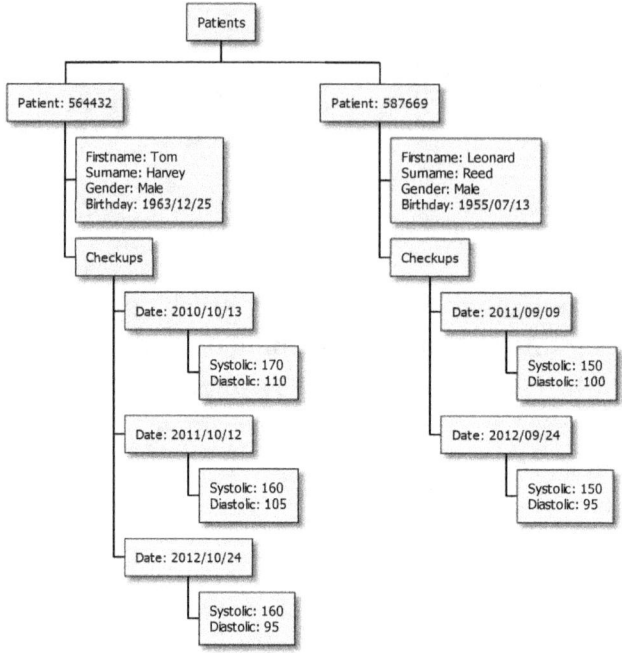

Figure 4: Document Structure.

It is a convenient way to keep certain data in one place, but the hierarchy comes with downsides. Imagine medical staff involved in four out of five checkups. Where would that data be stored? The same employee would occur in four different locations in the document. Keeping data in a strictly hierarchical structure is not the most convenient.

6.2 NoSQL

These document structures can be very powerful for diverse types of data. Managing and accessing those structures and having redundant data for performance reasons requires custom software to access the data. There are many technical structures in NoSQL (Not Only SQL). For illustration purposes, we'll highlight the entity-attribute-value store as an example.

The Entity-Attribute-Value (EAV) model represents a data model designed to store sparse data efficiently. It is very convenient when storage space is at a premium or when runtime usage patterns are unpredictable and subject to continuous changes (imagine ever-growing variations of products sold on a merchant website).

Entity	Attribute	Value
{patient 564432}	Firstname	Tom
{patient 564432}	Surname	Harvey
{patient 564432}	Gender	Male
{patient 564432}	Birthday	1963/12/25
{patient 564432}	Checkup	2010/10/13
{patient 564432, 2010/10/13}	Systolic	170
{patient 564432, 2010/10/13}	Diastolic	110

Figure 5: NoSQL Structure.

Utilizing the data in a structure like that requires knowledge of how this data is stored. We require lots of metadata and software to handle it correctly. The metadata is separated from the data and stored like data again. Variations of NoSQL implementations exist for different technical reasons, including how it is stored and handled. The technology provides very little clarity on how it represents the business information due to its heavy focus on technology.

Newer NoSQL products have added the SQL back to allow developers to access the data stored inside. It shows that the term 'No' is not the discriminator but how data is structured. The paradox in reality is that it initially seems very productive and flexible. Yet to manage it with software an increasing number of rules is required, and solutions then require an enormous investment in technological expertise. And the technical optimizations themselves only make sense once the business information is really understood.

6.3 Logical Structure

When relational databases came into play, storage was not cheap. To optimize for storage, the normalization rules came about to create consistency by removing redundancy.

We can present this type of data structure in a set of tables in which we store every piece of data without redundancy:

Patients:

Patient	Firstname	Surname	Gender	Birthday
564432	Tom	Harvey	Male	1963/12/25
587669	Leonard	Reed	Male	1955/07/13

Checkups:

Patient No	Checkup	Systolic	Diastolic
564432	2010/10/13	170	110
587669	2011/09/08	150	95
564432	2011/10/12	150	105

Figure 6: Logical structure.

Since the data elements are grouped into tables, a more natural representation is to be found of what the business information beholds. However, be warned that even such an obvious-looking structure can be built very technical for optimization of all sorts, deviating again from the obvious meaning.

The advantages of this approach are that all similar data is only stored in one place, and managing the data is, therefore, less error-prone. The other advantage is the minimal storage requirements, though storage seems to become cheaper by the day. The downside of this 'store in one place' seems to be counterproductive when the data is shared across the globe and needs to be accessible in multiple places at the same time. Various database products exist nowadays to manage precisely that requirement and serve the need without losing the required integrity and data quality at scale.

6.4 Graph Structure

The graph paradigm abstracts all things to nodes and edges. The power and flexibility come with a labor-intensive approach requiring very specific technology. It does the opposite of the other variants. Instead of storing data in a very technical or organized manner, it stores every individual element in a very abstract structure as nodes and edges. For analytics and publishing purposes, it can be very instrumental in harmonizing varying data elements, definitions, and relations in such graphs.

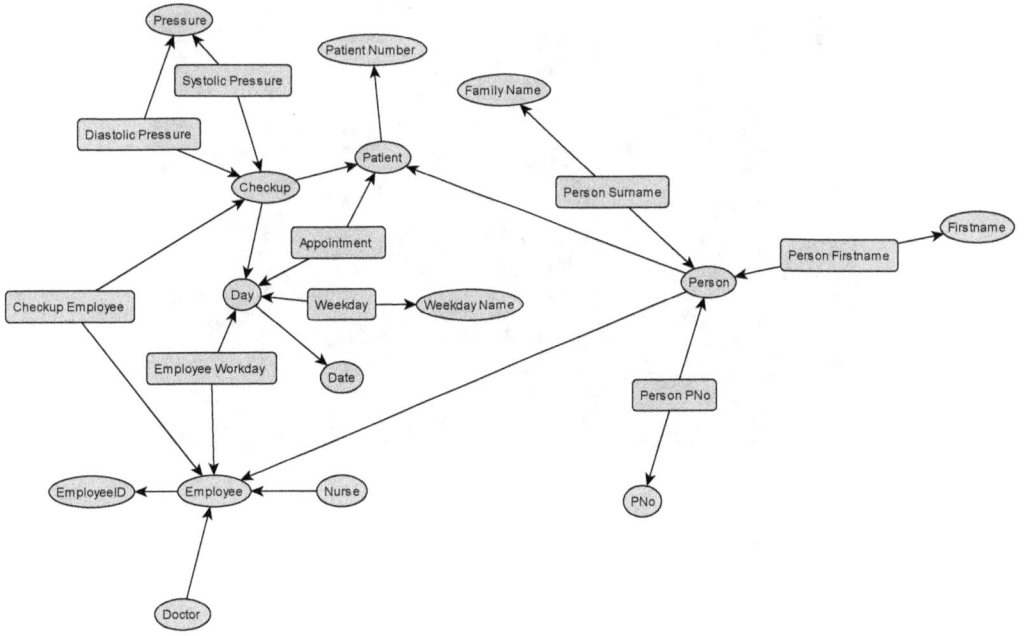

Figure 7: Graph structure.

Though not new, the acceptance of graphs by technology vendors and users is only now growing since more and more data needs to be integrated. Many solutions, however, still aim for information gathering and not yet for data storage. As with NoSQL, the accessibility is still very much done through non-SQL interfaces, making it hard for developers to use their known skillset.

7. Information Modeling

No matter the technology or data structure for storing and handling, it should always represent meaningful business information. Therefore, verbalizing, communicating, and verifying the data is crucial.

Viewing the business information from a non-technical viewpoint is as much a starting point as it is a finish line since all stakeholders involved must be able to communicate and participate.

7.1 Working with Facts

The absolute truth is a very hard thing to agree upon. There are too many perspectives to come up with a single truth. Just imagine how various departments of the organization deal with the concept of Customer. There simply is not a single version of a customer. However, we can agree upon facts about the customer, which can support many versions of truths. So, to start with what is unambiguous, we model facts. There's a simple three-step method to gather facts and build your model. These involve collecting, sorting, and analyzing.

7.1.1 Collecting Facts

To exchange data unambiguously, we need to be aware of the most significant data along with its context. Before we start modeling, we need to make sure the expressed facts are correct themselves. They should adhere to a set of rules. These rules emphasize the atomicity and concreteness of fact expressions. Here are examples of the most common patterns illustrating some rules:

Identifying something:

```
"Patient 659573 exists."
```

Identifying something and providing one value:

```
"Patient 659573 is called John."
```

Identifying something and identifying one other thing:

```
"Patient 659573 has a checkup on 01-01-2018."
```

In this patient record example (see Chapter 6, Figure 3), the Patient Numbers seem to be the most significant and unique piece of data to which all other data is related. Therefore, we cannot simply state "John is born 1963", since it would require more context to know which John we are talking about. So, we state the facts using expressions that include solid identification. In our example, we use the Patient Number. When expressing all data in language, we now include the proper identification of the facts:

```
"Patient 564432 is born on 1963/12/25."
"The first name of patient 564432 is Tom."
"The family name of patient 564432 is Harvey."
"The gender assigned at birth of patient 564432 is male."
"On 2010/10/13, patient 564432 has blood pressure 170/110."
```

7.1.2 Sorting Facts

By adding more facts from the second patient record, we can sort them on the type of fact they represent. Once that sorting completes, fact type names are provided:

Checkup:

```
"The patient 654432 has a checkup on 2010/10/13."
"The patient 587669 has a checkup on 2012/09/24."
```

Patient Firstname:

```
"The first name of patient 587669 is Leonard."
"The first name of patient 564432 is John."
```

7.1.3 Analyzing Facts

We can now start finding the Objects and Values within the sorted and named facts. We will select phrases to name objects or mark the final data values in that discovery process with the domain experts. The discovery and analysis are building the so-called information grammar. Most prominently, it helps us discover the objects, the things that have business meaning, and the values used in the universe of discourse to store the actual data in a system, and truly learn about the business knowledge.

7.1.4 Building Blocks

Most importantly, the building blocks of information models consist of facts, objects, and values. Next to those, there are business constraints, definitions, annotations, and more. We will get back to that in Chapter 8. But let's start with the most important parts first.

7.1.5 Values

Values are easy to find in the expressions, and we can list them in a table-like format. We refer to these as 'data'. We identify Patients by their Patient Numbers, which are just simple values.

```
Patient Number  First name   Gender type   Date
564432          John         Male          1963-12-25
587669          Leonard      Male          1955-07-13
```

The same goes for the First Name or the Gender Type. This table of data illustrates how easy it is to misunderstand it. In the example above, we see date values, yet there is not enough information to determine what kind of date they are. It requires a business term to provide context. In this case, it should've been *Birthdate*.

7.1.6 Objects

Object types are not the same as objects in the physical reality, but rather identifiable elements within our communication. The linguistic word nominalization means the naming of things, to make a noun. These nouns correspond to the so-called Objects. The Patient Number values are already visible in the data, but to communicate with context, we need phrases to communicate the Objects. Similar to the fact type names, we name these phrases or object types:

Patient

```
'patient 564432'
'patient 587669'
```

Also, a little less obvious at this point are the checkup days. These days are not just a collection of dates, for they hold special meaning in the world of patients, doctors, and checkups. We may store these days in a date format but behold more meaning to the business domain, as we will learn later.

Day

```
'2010/10/13'
'2011/10/12'
```

7.2 Information Grammar

Distinguishing the facts, objects, and values in our communication is essential for creating meaningful, verifiable, and reusable information. By re-using single points of definitions, we eliminate redundancy in knowledge and maintain a meaningful connection between all model elements. This interconnectedness will prove crucial as we delve further into the information modeling journey.

Facts consist of semantics and roles (placeholders) to our Objects and/or Values. In turn, the Objects may again contain semantics and Roles to more Objects and/or Values. We call the structure of these relations hard semantics, whereas the text phrases are called soft semantics. Separating those two aspects allows easy translation without losing meaning or context, as demonstrated in Paragraph 13.7. By graphically displaying the fact, objects, and their values, we can observe how the collection of data is communicated in language:

Patient Firstname:
"Patient 587669 is called Leonard."

The double underline distinguishes objects and the single distinguishes values. Graphically, this can be depicted to also allow the naming of Objects and Values. The graphical rendering of information grammar:

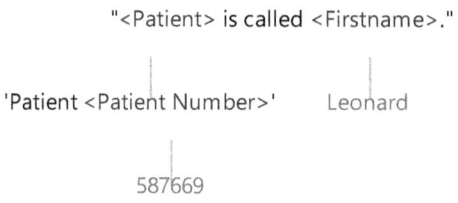

Figure 8: Patient Firstname grammar.

Let's provide another fact expression that expresses the checkup of a patient on a specific day:

Checkup:
"The patient 587669 has a checkup on 2012/09/24."

By modeling the object 'patient 587669', we can establish information structures and share the common object types. This highlights the interconnectedness of the information model, allowing for a comprehensive understanding of the relationships between different elements. Only by naming the types in conjunction with domain experts, do we discover and learn the existence of Patient, Checkup Day, and Day. Using the information grammar, one can see how the expression communicates using a structure containing objects and values.

Having stated the above form for most rules, deviations are common. When two things are related, the things (or objects) may be a nested set of objects and values. This is a very powerful function of building full information model structures.

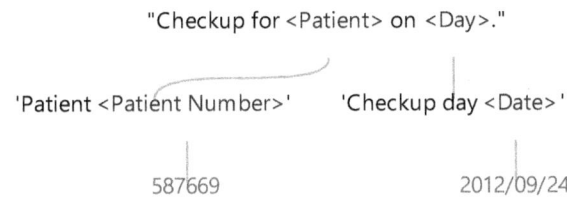

Figure 9: Patient Checkup Day grammar.

Take, for example, the result of the employee who performed the actual checkup.

"<u>Employee 465</u> performed <u>checkup for patient 587669 on checkup day 2011/09/09</u>."

It speaks of employee, checkup, and patient. Below is the fact expression and the information grammar:

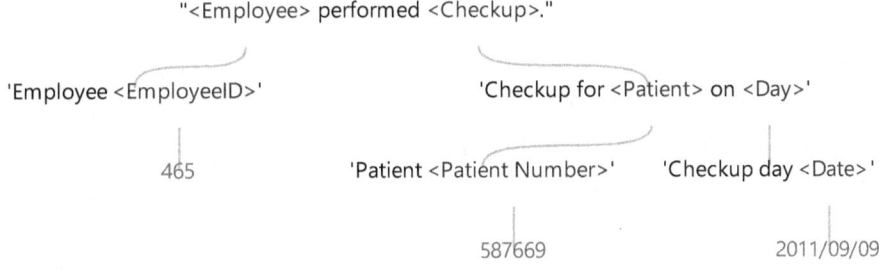

Figure 10: Employee Checkup grammar.

7.3 Objects can be Facts

As you have seen in the previous paragraph, we can verbalize facts and recognize objects. This does not prevent us from also stating facts about objects. This flexibility of language is very powerful in communication and in the information modeling realm.

Patient Checkup:

"Patient 659573 has a checkup on 01-01-2018."

Employee Checkup:

"Employee 465 did the checkup on patient 587669 on 2011/09/09."

The first expression states a fact for the patient checkup. The second fact expresses which employee performed the patient checkup. In conclusion, the patient checkup is stated as a fact, but simultaneously referred to as an object in the second fact.

Grammars from Figure 9 and Figure 10 can be folded into one information model, whereas facts can also be referenced as objects.

The repurposing of facts as object types lead us to the statement by Harm van der Lek: "Objects are in fact also facts.". The consequence of this mathematical insight becomes very powerful in building automation. This will be made clearer in Chapters 11 and Chapter 12.

7.4 Elementary Fact Expressions

Intuitively, you can now understand that facts should be concrete and atomic. Concrete means that expressions always contain values or data to illustrate the use of data.

Atomic means that there is no unnecessary information in the expression, and removing any part of it would result in a loss of meaning.

To illustrate, here are some **invalid** fact expressions:

7.4.1 Non-atomic Facts

Facts need to be atomic. We can exchange facts, but for the sake of information modeling, we should express atomic facts. The smallest fact expressible means one cannot leave out information without losing meaning. Similarly, every expression should only contain a single fact.

```
"Patient 659573 has first name Tom and surname Harvey."
"Both patient 659573 and 659574 have surname Harvey."
```

As you can see, both expressions contain multiple facts. We should rephrase these to consist of only a single fact per expression, as shown in the previous paragraphs. Consistently ask yourself, can I break my expression into two or more facts?

7.4.2 Non-concrete Facts

Facts expressed need to be concrete with real examples for domain experts to verify them. Even though speaking of object types can be very efficient in communicating, there is also a serious risk of being misunderstood. As you may read below:

```
"The patient has a first name."
"A patient has a checkup on 01-01-2018."
```

Both facts above may be true, but neither holds any value since we cannot say which facts it really concerns. Which patient are we talking about?

7.4.3 Non-unique Facts

Again, facts need to be unique. This means the values mentioned in the expressions must be unique instances. There may be many Toms, or even multiple Tom Harvey's, within our records. Although our expressions may be true, are our facts uniquely identifiable?

```
"Tom is male."
"Tom Harvey has a checkup on 01-01-2018."
```

7.4.4 Different Words, Same Facts

It is worth noting that we can use different verbalizations to express the same fact, which are all valid at the same time. For example:

```
"Patient 659573 has a checkup on 01-01-2018."
"On 01-01-2018, patient 659573 has a checkup."
"The checkup on 01-01-2018 is for patient 659573."
```

By adhering to these ground rules, fact expressions can accurately represent information concisely and meaningfully.

This chapter has laid the foundation for understanding fact expressions in information modeling. We can accurately state facts and avoid ambiguity by ensuring that expressions are atomic and concrete. We have explored various examples and identified the ground rules for correct fact expressions. Going forward, the book will utilize a graphical representation to depict fact expressions, allowing for a visual understanding of their relationships and structure. This graphical approach will enhance our comprehension and enable effective information modeling.

One can easily see how different languages can verbalize the same facts, as another illustration shows how soft semantics are required to communicate to the stakeholder in their own language and the need for solid structures, which are the hard semantics. International organizations often need to speak localized facts and facts in a globally agreed-upon language. Being able to separate the hard and soft semantics makes perfect sense.

7.5 Facts in Text and Diagram

So far, we've seen data verbalized in natural language and shown information grammar structures. This is very powerful in analyzing fact expressions, but we need something more when it comes to a full information model. Before continuing, please take a moment to digest the following graphical representations of the same single fact.

Checkup:
  "Patient 587669 has a checkup on day 2012/09/24."

This fact appears as a grammar in Figure 11, and we can depict it graphically to combine all available knowledge embedded in it. The diagram depicts the grammar examples and symbols for Fact (Checkup), Object (Patient and Checkup Day), and Value Types (Patient Number, Day):

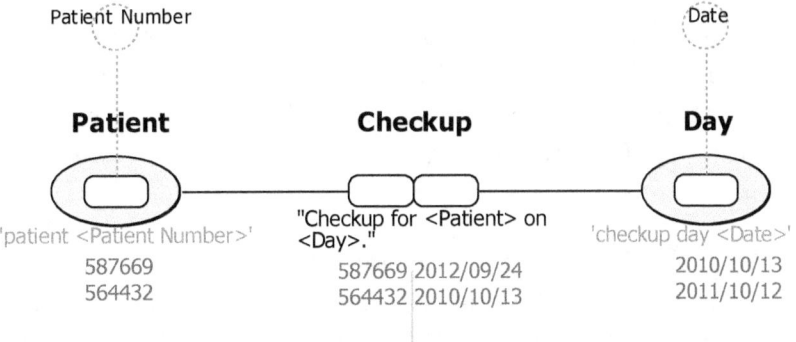

Figure 11: Fact, grammar, and diagram.

7.6 Values Matter

We are comfortable efficiently communicating at type levels. We talk about things like "a customer buys an article." Communicating at a type-level works if everyone involved implies the same context. This proves very hard when stakeholders have different professions and come with different world views. We assume we share the same worldview and, therefore, have the same context. Concrete examples are sometimes required to verify whether we communicate within the same context.

If we speak of a pipe, we all have an image of a pipe in our minds. However, the picture is not an actual pipe. And since we each have a different picture in our mind, modeling pipes can be ambiguous. With the word pipe, we need to provide a concrete example of the pipe we are talking about to verify if we have the same understanding.

The following dialog between medical staff illustrates that we can communicate on an abstract type level, but we always need to be exact if we want to verify the data being communicated. This is where concrete examples come in.

I have a **patient** with a high fever.
Which **patient**?
Ah, I am talking about <u>patient 465756</u>.
What is this **patient's** temperature?
It is almost <u>120 degrees</u>!
That can't be right, he'd be boiling!
Oh, sorry, I meant <u>40 degrees Celsius</u>.
Now I see. Give the **patient** 250mg of paracetamol and call me again if the temperature does not drop in the next 20 minutes. And please be more clear next time.
Will do, next time I'll communicate more clearly, such as: **"Patient 465756 has a temperature of 40 degrees Celsius."**
That'd be great! It saves us time, prevents miscommunication, and results in a better treatment for our **patient**.

Figure 12: Dialog starting abstract and getting concrete.

Another example to illustrate the need for concrete values to validate information in our communication is when we are modeling an inventory. Even though everyone in a meeting may agree upon the definition, only the actual values will illustrate if we are considering the same things. As displayed in this miscommunication:

Inventory: A comprehensive list or record of goods, assets, or resources that an organization, business, or individual holds in stock.

```
John (sales):
   "We have 25 articles with article number 4059."

 Mary (purchase):
   "We have 19 articles with article number 4059."

 Jack (storage):
   "We have 6 articles with article number 4059."
```

Figure 13: Inventory counts.

Examples help verify if the experts are talking about the same thing. Clearly, inventory was too generic and lacked context from the different business domains. Better would've been the Inventory Available, Articles Ordered, and Articles Reserved to be able to calculate the right amounts and consider ordered articles, which are not yet delivered, reserved articles, which are not yet shipped, and the physical articles on the shelves.

It is easy to think each word needs a definition, but truly validating the meaning of the word and its definition requires examples as well. These examples are not needed to explain the wording, but to verify with all readers we're really talking about the same thing. With examples, we are now able to illustrate how it is applied in our business information, and it becomes easy to illustrate what it should not be. Next is an example of how to clearly not talk about our patients:

Patient First Name:

```
"Patient in bed 1 is called Captain Jack."
```

8. Information Constraints

In this chapter, we explore the world of constraints in information modeling, which are the foundational rules that govern information integrity. These constraints lay the groundwork for a structured and reliable information ecosystem. To comprehensively understand this topic, we journey through the most prevalent types of constraints, examining their roles and significance.

We describe basic constraints that help us identify things, state what is mandatory, provide consistency, and enable modelers to document rules and regulations that lack graphical representations. These constraints will guide our business exploration, shed light on the domain at hand, and steer artifact generation, as described in Chapter 12.

8.1 Unique Occurrences

In the domain of patients, we refer to patients using their Patient Numbers. These numbers need to be unique for all patients. In other words, we identify each patient with a unique Patient Number. Similarly, we identify each Day with a unique Date. Also, every Checkup contains a unique combination of a Patient and a Day. When stating the following unique constraints:

```
Every patient is identified by a unique Patient Number.
Every Checkup Day is identified by a unique Day.
```

```
Every Checkup is identified by a unique combination of Patient
    and Day.
```

We visualize these unique constraints graphically with horizontal lines over the relevant Roles in Figure 14. The fact-oriented modeling method rules state the so-called **N Rule** (N representing the number of roles) for objects. This is a rule of thumb, as we can see later in Paragraph 13.2, yet there are again, exceptions to the rule.

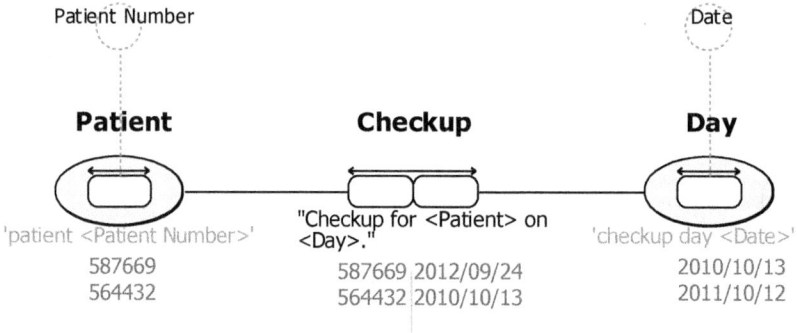

Figure 14: Patient and checkup day identifiers.

Similarly, the **N-1 Rule** applies for fact types. In a fact type with N roles, a uniqueness constraint must exist over at least N-1 roles. Figure 15 illustrates that patients can occur only once in Patient Surname.

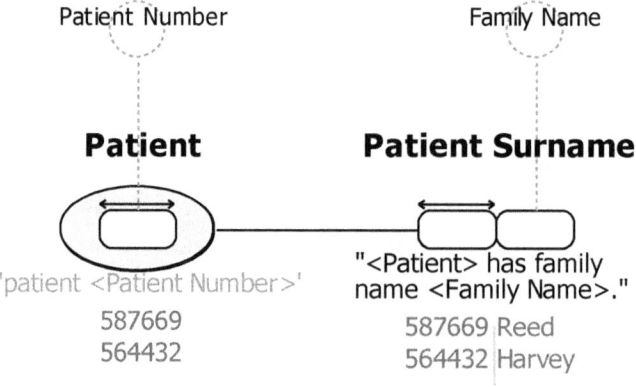

Figure 15: patient surname identify diagram.

Patient Surname is identified by the Patient, resulting in the rule that a Patient can only have one Surname.

Patient Surname

```
"Patient 587669 has family name Reed."
"Patient 564432 has family name Harvey."
```

The constraints help us to conclude that the following set of facts for Patient Surname is NOT valid:

```
"Patient 587669 has family name Reed."
"Patient 587669 has family name Harvey."
"Patient 587669 has family name Smith."
```

Even for more complex expressions, these N-Rule and N-1 Rule, still apply:

```
"Employee 465 performed checkup for patient 587669 on checkup
   day 2011/09/09."
```

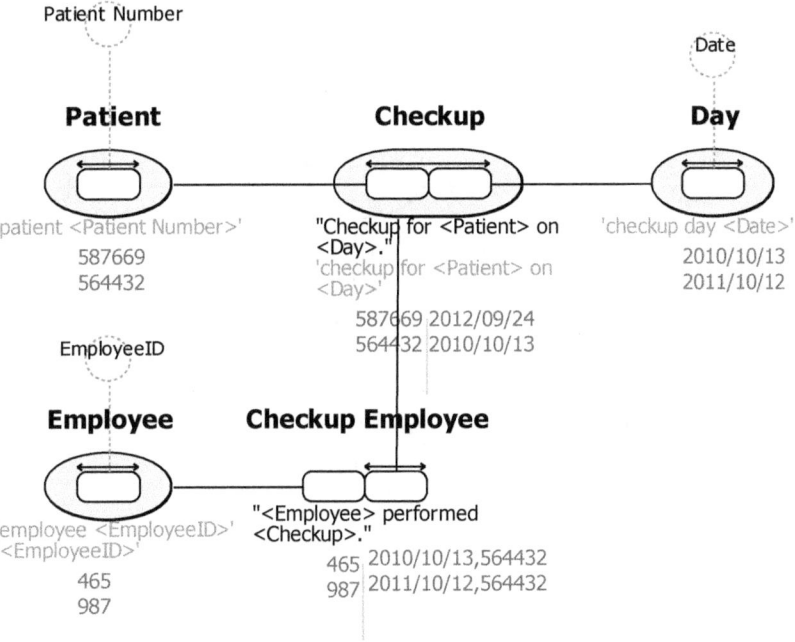

Figure 16: Facts comply to the N-1 rule.

Each Checkup Employee must have a unique Checkup. We conclude there cannot be two employees at the same checkup. This constraint not only tells how to identify object types, but also reflects how the business states what can and cannot occur. The unique constraints steer the generation of logical models, as shown in paragraph 11.5 Rules Drive the logical model.

8.2 Mandatory Occurrences

Totality constraints are another important aspect of information modeling. These constraints ensure that a population, or a set of entities, must exist within a specific context. Let's explore this further in the context of patient registration.

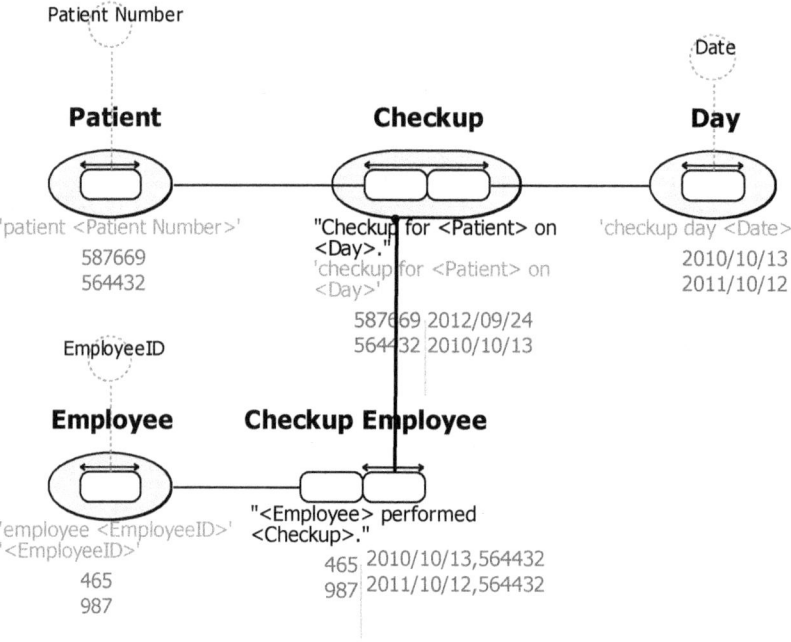

Figure 17: Graphical presentation of a mandatory constraint.

One **implicit** constraint in patient registration is that every registered patient must have a Patient Number. This constraint is guaranteed by the Patient having only one role to Patient Number. We can only communicate about Patient using their unique Patient Number.

We can also establish **explicit** constraints to enforce specific requirements. The business states every Checkup must be performed by an Employee. This is visualized by the mandatory constraint (dot and thick line) from Checkup to the Checkup Employee. It is verbalized as every population in Checkup must also exist in the population of Checkup Employee.

Mandatory constraints are transformed into database table columns to be nullable or not. However, when they are involved in a relationship or foreign key, they specify cardinalities on relationships to document the minimal occurrence of one (See also Paragraph 9.2).

8.3 Limit Occurrence Values

The value constraint restricts the possible values for a specific label type. Let's consider the following fact expression:

Checkup Result:

> "Checkup of Patient 587669 on 09-09-2011 shows hypertension."

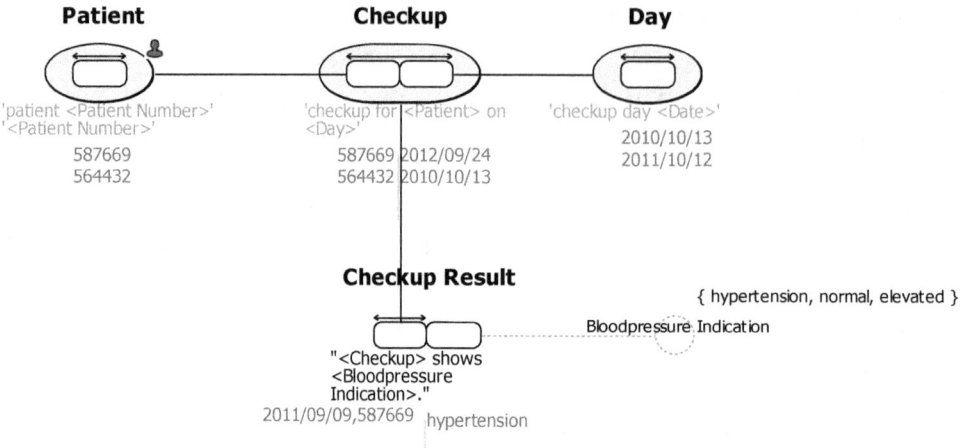

Figure 18: Graphical representation of value constraints.

The blood pressure result can only be one of three indications: elevated, hypertension, or normal.

8.4 Consistent Occurrences

The subset constraint allows modelers to state that a particular population must occur elsewhere. This can be compared to foreign keys in databases, where the presence of a value in one table depends on its occurrence in another table. The difference with actual foreign keys, is that these types of constraints may result in a database check constraint instead. In the context of information modeling, subset constraints operate on the roles within fact types.

We are given the business constraint that every patient needs an appointment before coming in for a checkup. We state that the population of Checkup must exist in the population of Appointment, as visualized in the figure below:

Appointment:

> "Patient 587669 has an appointment for checkup day 2011/09/09."

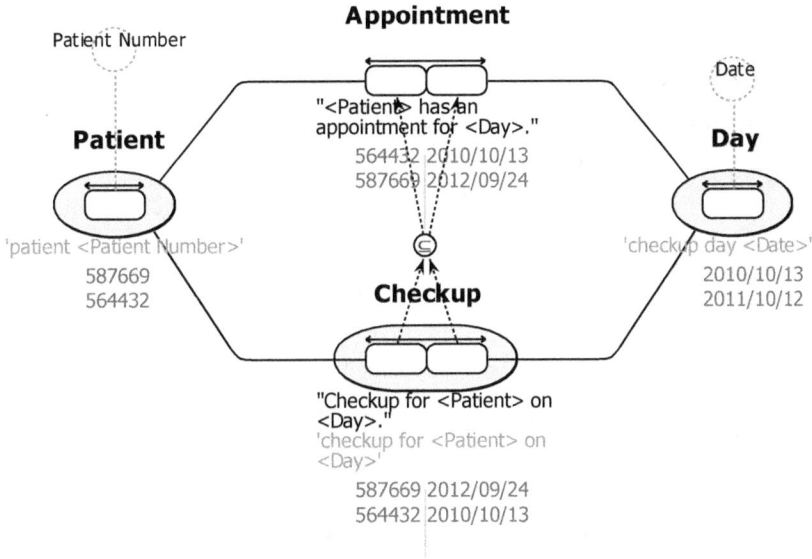

Figure 19: Consistency across facts.

Subset constraints are useful for maintaining referential integrity and ensuring that we properly enforce data dependencies within an information model.

8.5 Counting Occurrences

The cardinality constraint specifies the number of occurrences or instances allowed for a relationship between two object types. It defines the numerical limits or range of instances that can exist in a specific relationship.

In a hypothetical case where the business allows no more than five checkups, we could add a cardinality constraint limiting the occurrences of patients in the total collection of checkups.

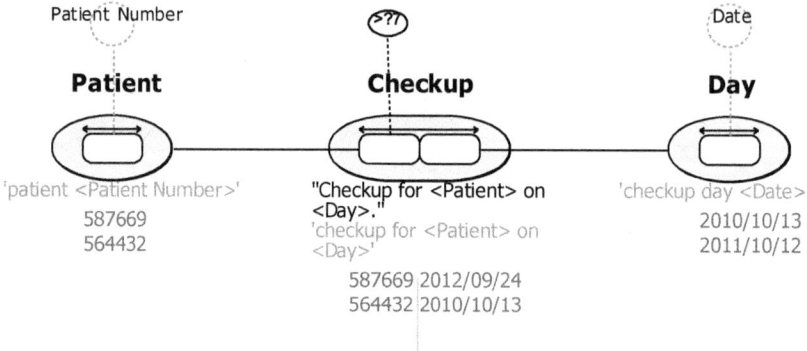

Figure 20: Limiting the amount of facts.

8.6 One Occurrence and not the Other

We use the exclusive constraint to specify that certain options or values within an attribute or relationship are mutually exclusive. This means that only one option or value can be selected or applied at a time.

In our domain, doctors are authorized to speak to patients about the plans for treatment and make decisions about it, whereas nurses are usually the more hands-on employees. We added an exclusion constraint to ensure the employees are not listed as both. With the exclusion constraint, we can formalize that an employee can be a doctor or a nurse, but not both.

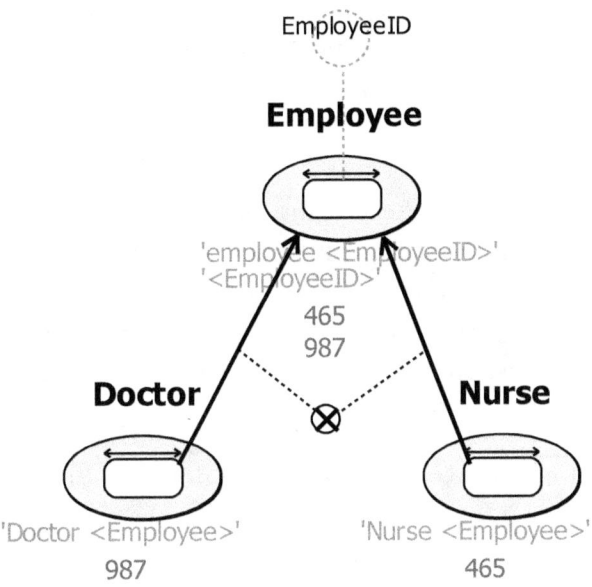

Figure 21: Employees can be a doctor or a nurse.

8.6.1 Subtype

Another thing to notice in the previous diagram is that the lines are now thicker and contain an arrow. These indicate the Doctor is a special employee, as is the Nurse. In other words, the Doctor and the Nurse are subtypes of the Employee. They share the same identification and when it is time to introduce facts related to the Employee, these fact types also automatically apply to the Doctor and Nurse. More on this topic under 10.2 Taxonomies.

8.7 Miscellaneous

In this chapter, we covered the constraints supported by most technological artifacts. There are countless more business constraints. More advanced rules require more sophistication and usually more coding by developers. To not overload the domain expert with technical constructs, simply documenting these rules will suffice in most cases, since they need to be specified and verified by domain experts.

For more information on various types of models and business documentation, please look at Chapter 9.

9. Diagrams

Diagrams play a crucial role in visually representing the information structure of a model. They provide a way for modelers to comprehend and analyze the information model more effectively.

The purpose of diagrams is to draw attention to specific areas or aspects within the overall information model. For example, you can create a diagram specifically focused on patient information, gathering all the relevant elements related to patients. Similarly, you can create another diagram for medication information, capturing the elements specific to medications. These diagrams allow you to isolate and highlight areas of interest while still maintaining the interconnectedness of all elements within the complete information model.

By utilizing diagrams, modelers can gain a visual understanding of the information structure, facilitating comprehension, analysis, and communication of the model. Diagrams serve as a valuable tool in representing and exploring different aspects of the information model, enabling modelers to focus on specific domains or entities as needed.

Many tools use diagramming as a way to model. The diagram, therefore, becomes synonymous with the model itself. The FCO-IM method, however, models the communication and therefore considers diagrams to be merely a visual representations of relevant parts of the information model.

9.1 FCO-IM Diagram

In the *Fully Communication Oriented Information Modeling* approach, an FCO-IM diagram is a visualization and can serve as a reference for other types of diagrams, such as Relational, UML Class Diagrams, Concept Maps, etc.

The purpose of the FCO-IM diagram is to provide a visual representation of the information model based on the communication and fact expressions discussed earlier, including the richness in constraints and annotations. The FCO-IM diagram captures the essential elements of the information model and their relationships.

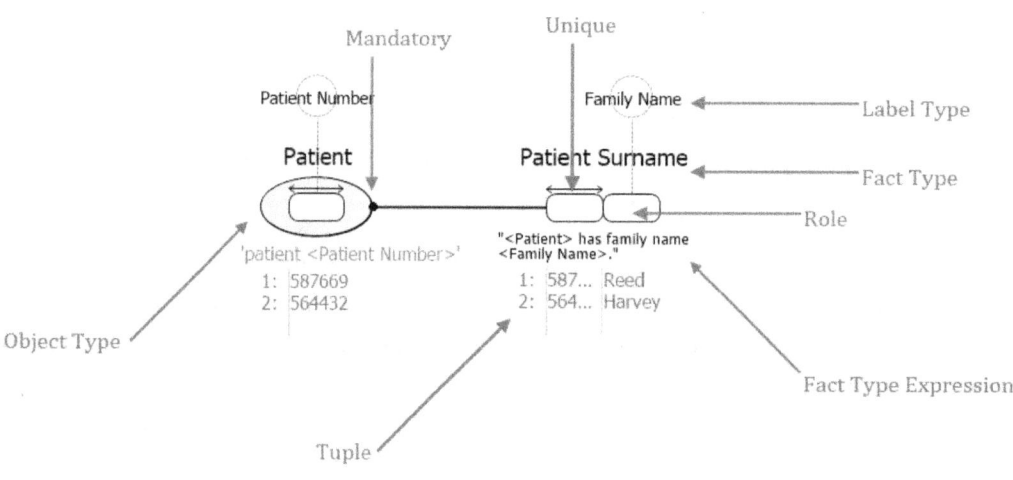

Figure 22: FCO-IM diagram explained.

By visualizing the information model in an FCO-IM diagram, modelers can gain insights into the underlying structure and make informed decisions when mapping it to other diagramming notations or implementing it in different systems or databases. The FCO-IM diagram serves as a visual for further analysis, design, and development activities.

9.2 Relational Diagram

The relational diagram serves as a visual representation of the logical model of a database. It captures the structure of the database tables, their attributes, and the relationships between them. Traditionally, database design follows a top-down approach through the conceptual, logical, and physical data model (see Figures 23 and 24).

When we create the physical data model, all many-to-many relations and data types are to be visualized. This will create more details and more tables.

Logical or relational modeling is the most widely adopted and supported data modeling approach. It's well-documented and has extensive tool support. It promotes data normalization, which reduces data redundancy and enforces data integrity, making it easier to maintain and query data. Data in a relational database is typically more consistent and can enforce referential integrity through foreign keys. Information models can easily derive these requirements. See Chapter 11.

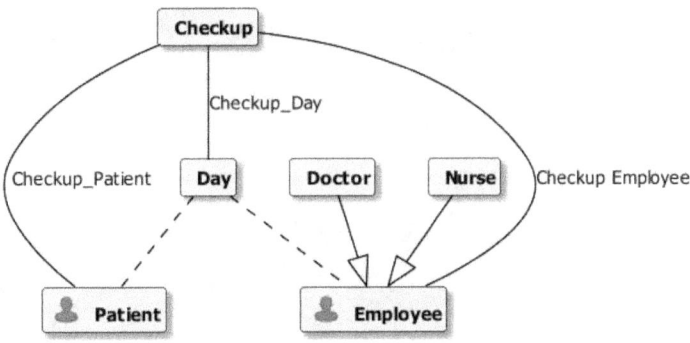

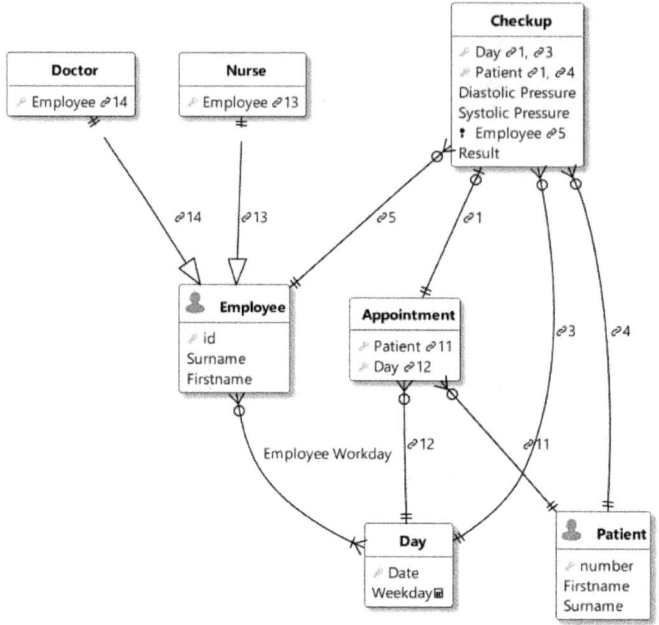

Figure 23: Conceptual and logical data model.

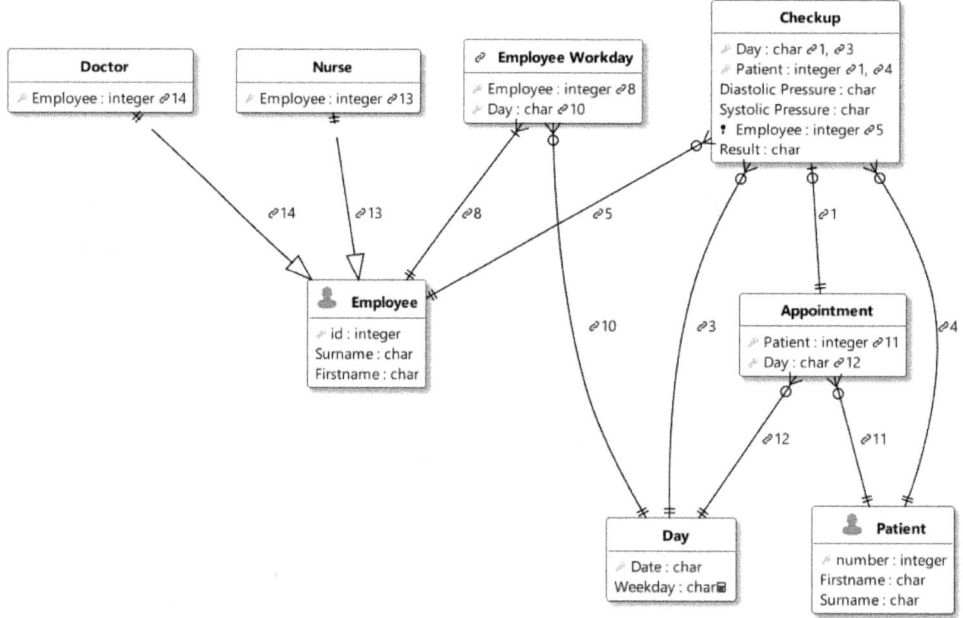

Figure 24: Physical data model.

However, all the above data models lack semantics. Adding verbs to the relationships instead of showing relationship numbers is still insufficient to fully grasp the original facts.

CaseTalk offers the advantage of generating these data models directly from the original information model and extending them with fact expressions (See Figure 25). This saves time and ensures consistency between the information model and the Relational diagrams. You might be surprised to read that all diagrams in this book come out of the box for free from an information model in CaseTalk.

Representing complex real-world relationships and facts can be challenging in a purely relational model. This can lead to convoluted schemas and complex queries in code. Traditional relational models can be less flexible when handling changes in data requirements. Modifying the schema often requires careful planning and may disrupt existing systems. Relational models can be less intuitive for non-technical stakeholders, making facilitating collaboration between different teams harder.

Depicting database views in correspondence to the Objects in the information model, which are absorbed into normalized tables as columns, can still be made visual using a special symbol and shown as database views. Note in Figure 26 how the Firstname and Surname of Person end up as columns in both the Employee and Patient tables, and we can still generate a database view to collect that data in a view.

In summary, the choice between fact-oriented information modeling and logical or relational modeling depends on the specific requirements. Fact-oriented modeling is more suitable for complex, dynamic domains and better for business process alignment. In contrast, logical or relational modeling is more widespread, provides strong data integrity, and may be preferred in environments where existing database technology and expertise are crucial. It's not uncommon for organizations to use a combination of both approaches to address different aspects of their data modeling requirements.

Traditional logical diagrams do not show subset constraints, table classifications, custom annotations, facts, or examples.

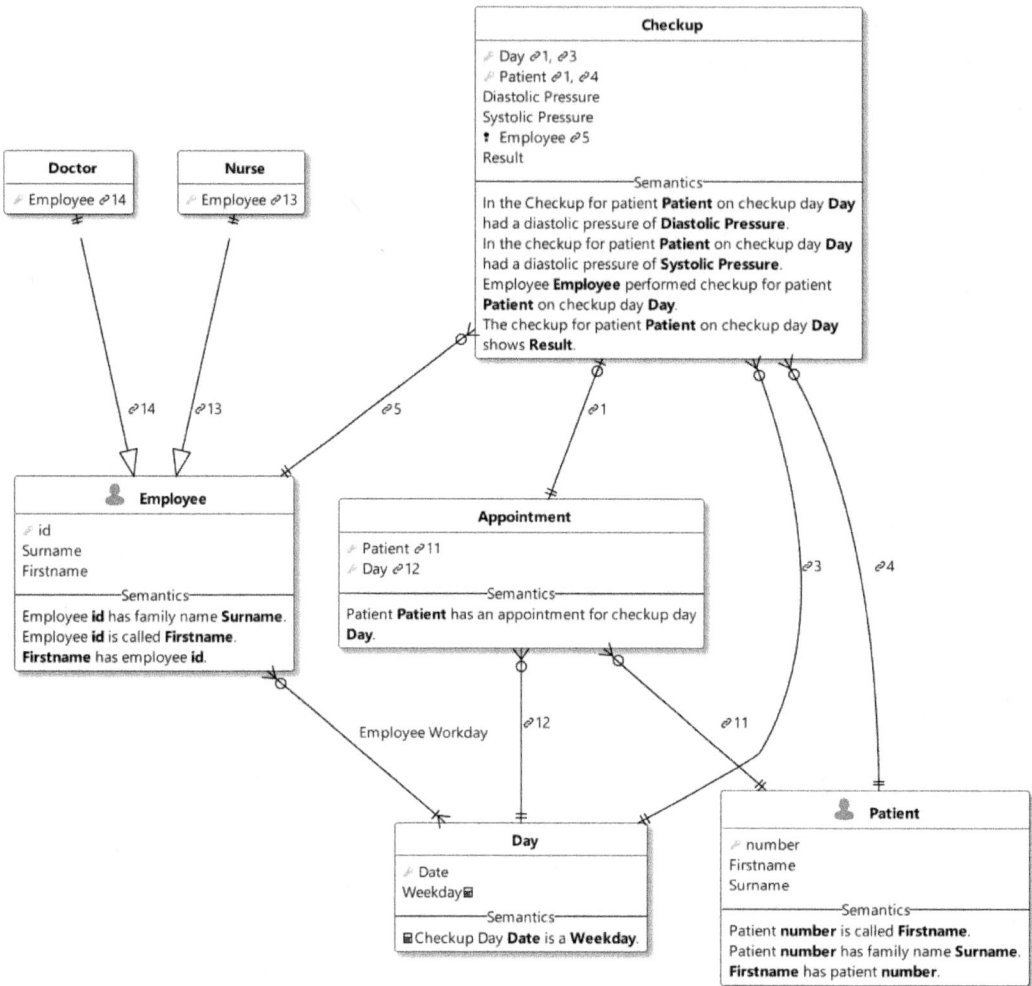

Figure 25: Logical data model with fact expressions.

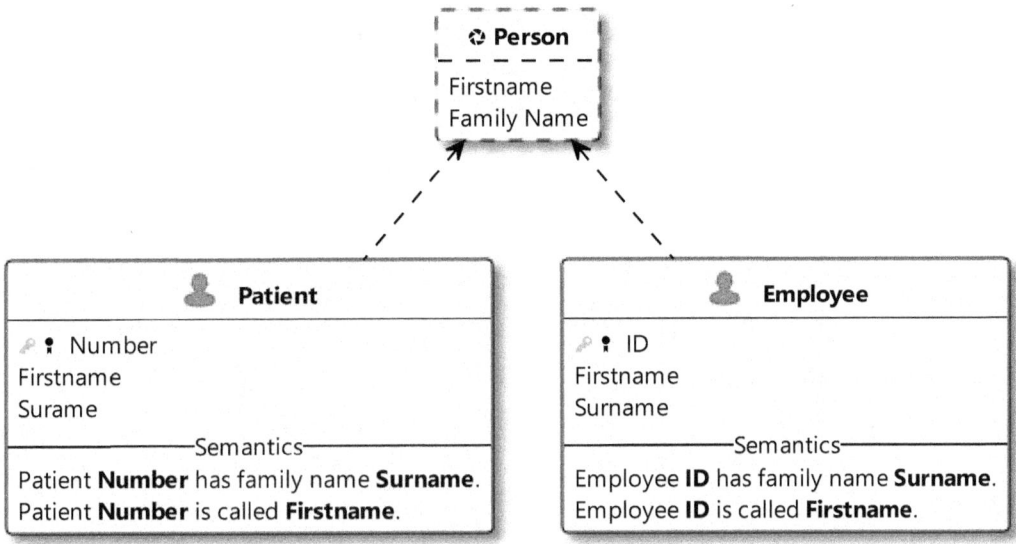

Figure 26: Database views to visualize object types.

9.3 UML Class Diagram

UML is a widely accepted industry standard for modeling software systems, making finding tools, resources, and expertise easy. UML class diagrams allow for the abstraction and modular representation of system components, making it easier to manage complex software systems. UML class design enforces data typing, which can help prevent data type-related errors in software development. UML class diagrams seamlessly integrate with object-oriented programming languages, facilitating software development and code-generation.

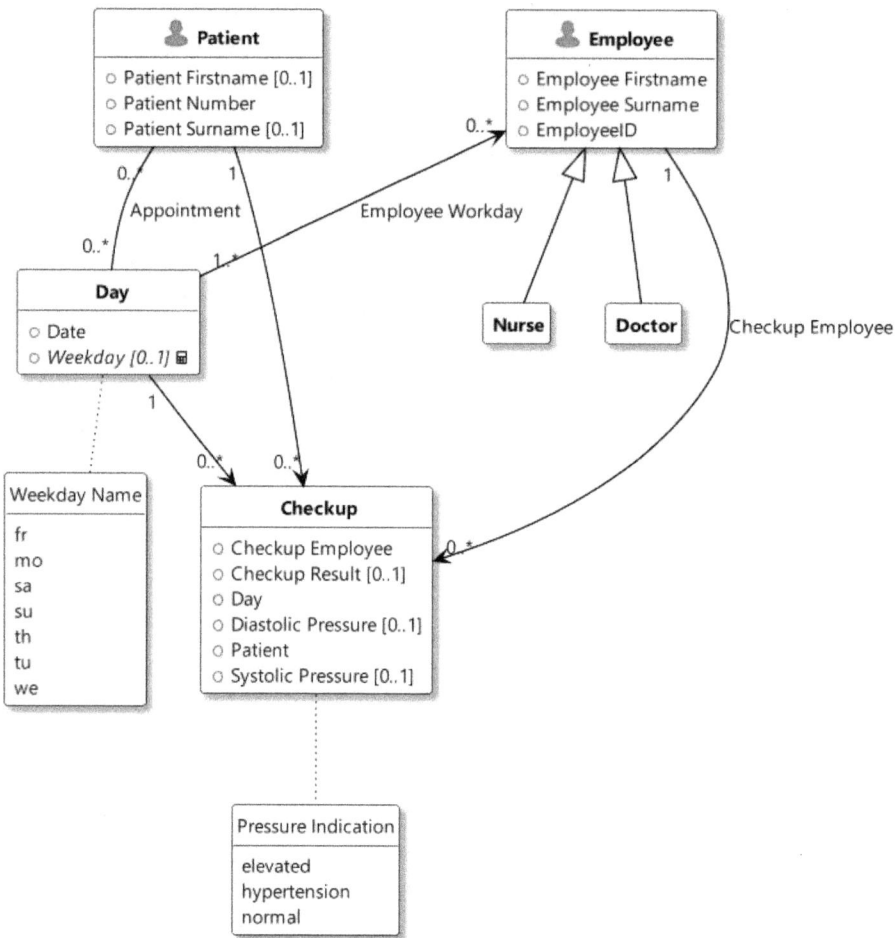

Figure 27: UML class diagram.

UML diagrams can be challenging for non-technical stakeholders to understand, potentially hindering effective communication between business and technical teams. UML class design can be rigid and less adaptable to changes in data structure or business rules, requiring careful planning for modifications. UML class diagrams primarily focus on software design and may not capture business semantics as effectively as fact-oriented modeling.

INFORMATION MODELING • 83

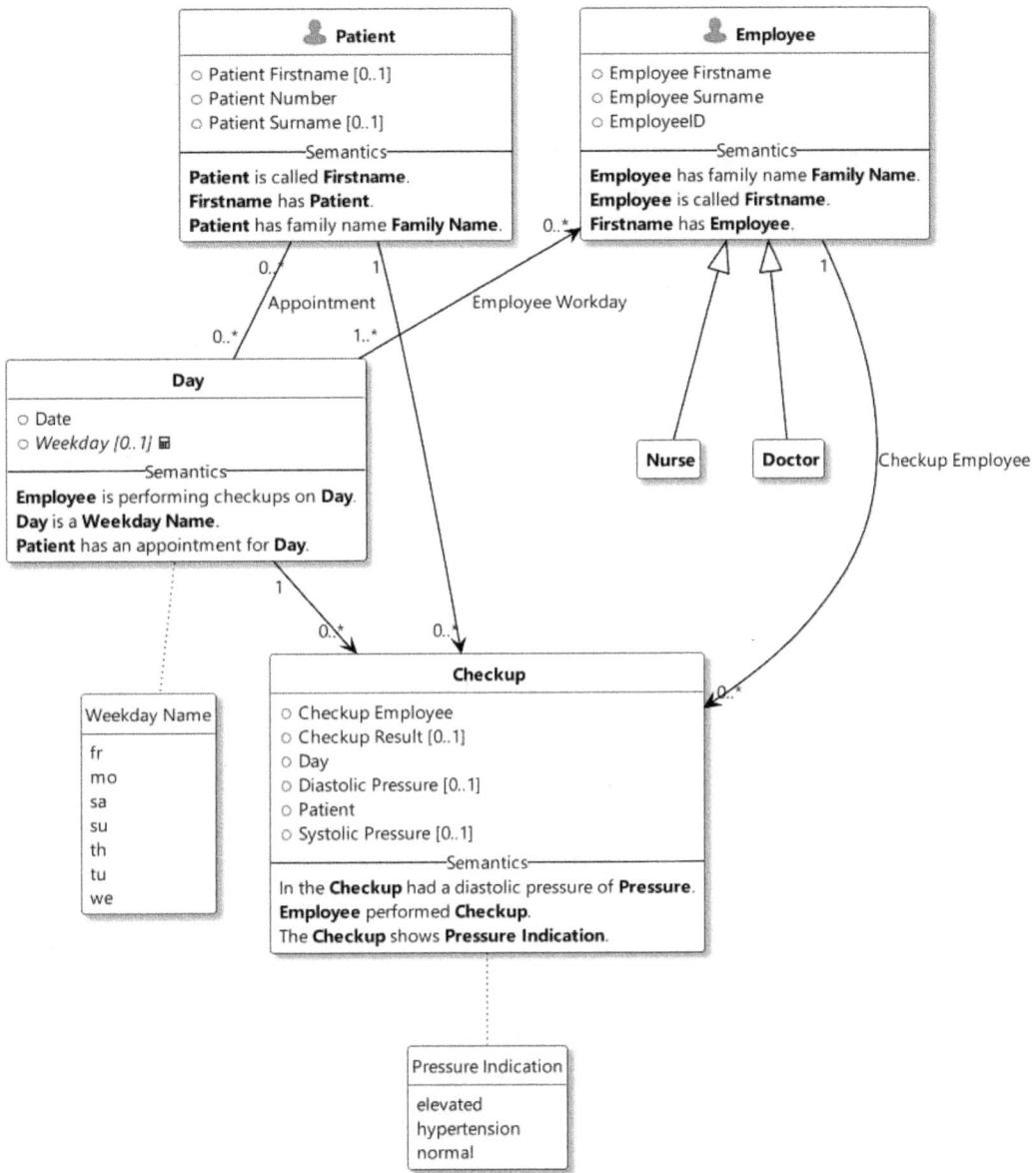

Figure 28: UML class diagram with fact expressions.

In summary, choosing between fact-oriented modeling and UML class design depends on the specific project requirements. Fact-oriented modeling is more suitable for complex, dynamic domains and aligning with business processes, whereas UML class design is a well-established software design and development choice. Organizations often use a combination of these modeling approaches to address different aspects of their data and software modeling needs.

UML Class diagrams do not show uniqueness constraints on the model. And like the relational diagrams, some constraints cannot be depicted in the diagram. Compared to relational diagrams, UML has the advantage of visualizing multi-value attributes and enumerations to list possible values.

CaseTalk allows you to generate UML Class Diagrams from the information model, enabling you to bridge the gap between the conceptual model and the software design phase. The UML Class Diagram derived from CaseTalk captures the classes, their properties, associations, and inheritance relationships based on the information model.

9.4 Concept Map

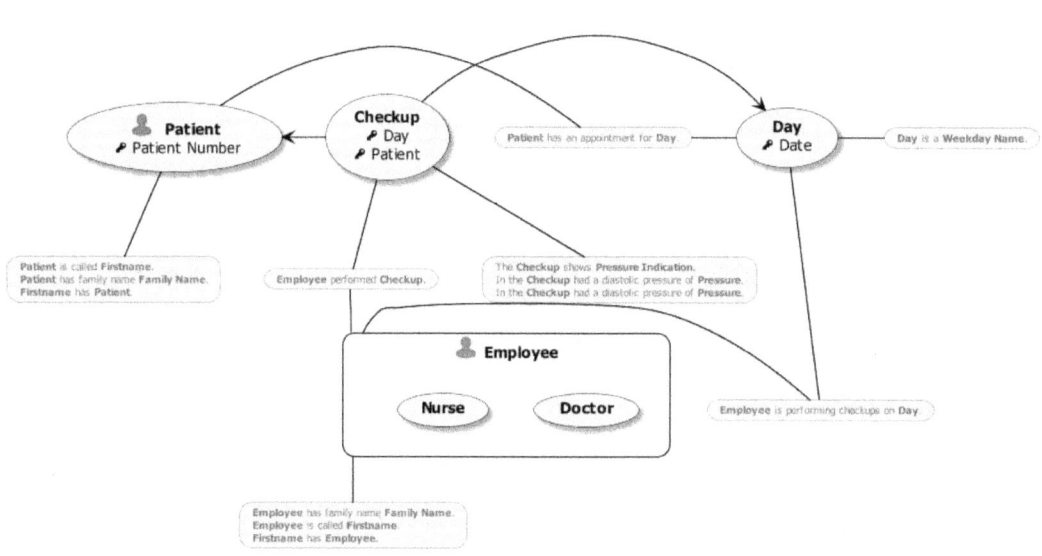

Figure 29: Concept map with fact expressions.

A concept map can help identify the various contextual aspects to consider when defining facts. Concept maps can help define the scope of the project or system. By identifying the core concepts and relationships, you can determine what aspects of the domain are in scope and which are out of scope, helping to manage project boundaries. As the requirements-gathering process progresses, a high-level concept map can evolve and be refined. It can serve as a living document that adapts to changing insights and requirements.

Incorporating a high-level concept map into the requirements-gathering process can be an essential bridge between business understanding and the subsequent fact-oriented modeling phase. It ensures that the facts captured in the models are grounded in the business domain and context, enhancing the accuracy and relevance of the resulting data models.

High-level concept maps can provide a visual representation of key concepts and their relationships. We've seen the result of that in Figure 29. These diagrams still lack fact expressions. When mixing them into the relationships and entities, the diagram may present a better overview.

10. Information Model Elements

The elements in information models can be numerous. We've seen the fact expressions using natural language and concrete examples. This is often a very powerful approach to make things clear and come to unambiguous communication, yet it is also a bottom-up approach. A different method of starting to scope the domain is a top-down approach. We can start from a high-level view in which concepts are first mentioned, classified, described, and documented. The following paragraphs show various elements useful in the top-down approach.

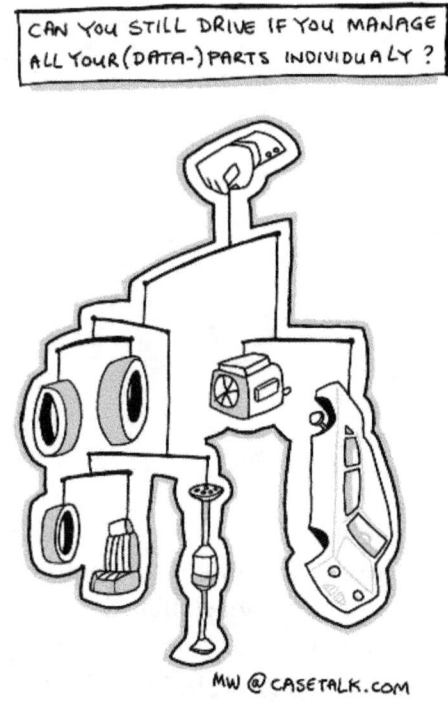

10.1 Containers and Concepts

In contrast to more technically intricate diagrams, a diagram with concepts are designed to convey a condensed, visually engaging, and easy-to-comprehend overview of the business needs. Its primary focus lies in accentuating the fundamental concepts or entities and the relationships that bind them, without delving into the intricacies of the underlying structure.

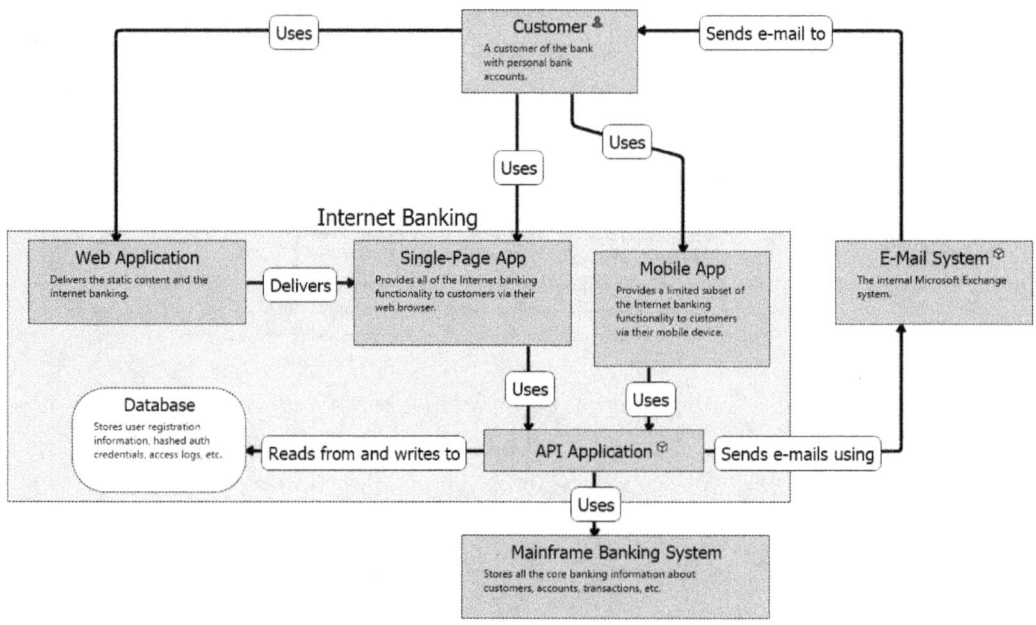

Figure 30: Diagram with concepts and containers.

Concepts and containers fulfill the vital role of providing a high-level perspective, promoting comprehension, and facilitating communication among non-technical stakeholders. By emphasizing the central entities and their connections, they empower business users to grasp the core of the information model without becoming entangled in technical specifics.

These high-level concepts can be linked to models, diagrams, related facts, objects, and values, allowing modelers to navigate and work top-down as well as bottom-up.

10.2 Taxonomies

Taxonomies, the organizational hierarchies of generalized and specialized entities, are pivotal structures in various domains. We can broadly classify them as either informal or formal taxonomies.

In an informal taxonomy, the structure resembles a classic classification system. Consider, for instance, a hierarchy that includes students, suppliers, and transportation companies. While it's evident that this hierarchy makes sense, there's an intriguing nuance to note. Different user groups may employ distinct criteria for identification. Students might use one set of identifiers, suppliers another, and transporting companies yet another. This divergence in identification methods characterizes an informal taxonomy. It's a flexible, adaptable way of classification that suits many scenarios.

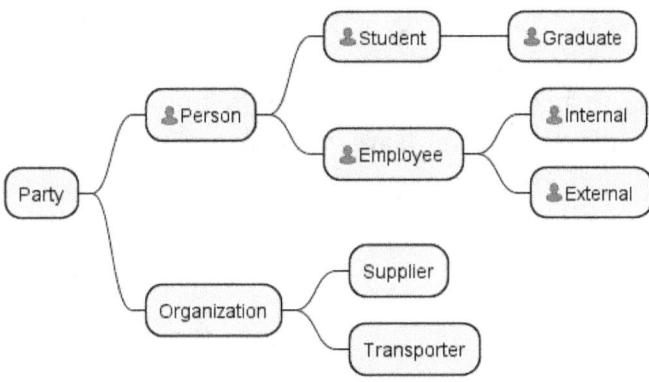

Figure 31: Informal taxonomy.

However, when dealing with data and information at scale, there arises a need for formal information models. These models demand that every element possesses a unique identifier. We consider only elements that share this identifier as specializations within the taxonomy. In this context, the hierarchy becomes more formal, with the unique identifier serving as a foundational element for classification. For example, all elements within the taxonomy could be categorized as "parties," each uniquely identified. This shift towards uniqueness and formality transforms the taxonomy into a formal one.

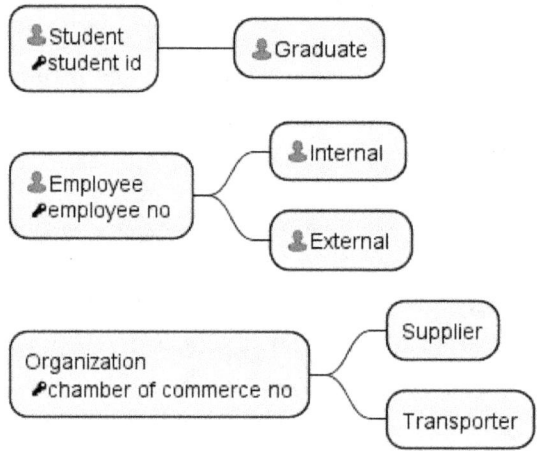

Figure 32: Formal taxonomy.

In summary, the distinction between informal and formal taxonomies hinges on the flexibility of identification methods. While informal taxonomies allow for varied identifiers, formal taxonomies necessitate a uniform, unique identification system to ensure precise and standardized data and information models.

10.3 Annotations

Annotations, manifesting as texts, definitions, and custom attributes on fact types, object types, and label types, play a pivotal role in enhancing the clarity, precision, and utility of information models. These textual elements serve as guiding beacons within the model, clarifying complex concepts, defining terms, and adding context. They act as a linguistic bridge that connects the technical intricacies of the model with the practical understanding of stakeholders.

Annotations in the form of texts and definitions provide in-depth insights, ensuring that entities and relationships are understood and interpreted uniformly across all parties. This standardized understanding is particularly valuable when dealing with stakeholders from diverse backgrounds, ensuring that no ambiguity or misunderstanding persists.

Custom attributes on fact types, object types, and label types offer a fine-tuned approach to model enrichment. They enable the incorporation of specific, context-sensitive information, allowing for tailored insights and the ability to capture unique details crucial for the model's relevance in the real world.

In summary, annotations are not just auxiliary notes within an information model; they are instrumental in bridging the gap between the technical aspects of the model and its real-world applicability. These annotations serve as compasses that steer the understanding of the model in the right direction, fostering efficient collaboration and enabling precise decision-making across diverse sets of stakeholders.

10.4 Paragraphs

In today's complex landscape of information modeling and data governance, we cannot overstate the need for well-structured documentation that seamlessly integrates various nested texts with references to elements in the information model. Such documentation acts as the backbone of effective communication, ensuring that all stakeholders, whether they possess a technical background or not, can grasp the intricacies of the model.

These (nested) texts serve multiple purposes, creating a holistic and clear understanding of the information model. They can encompass a myriad of sources, ranging from downloaded legal articles to manually crafted explanations. This diversity of content is essential for bridging the gap between technicalities and practical applicability.

The use of references, whether to elements within the model itself or external sources such as legal articles, reinforces the model's relevance and alignment with industry standards and regulations. This meticulous annotation process not only adds depth to the documentation but also enhances its transparency and credibility.

Moreover, these nested texts play a vital role in maintaining data integrity and upholding compliance with legal requirements. They help define the relationships and attributes within the model, ensuring that they adhere to the necessary legal frameworks.

In essence, this type of documentation is a dynamic tool that not only serves as a comprehensive guide to the information model, but also as a bridge between technical experts, business stakeholders, and legal frameworks. Its structured and layered approach fosters better understanding, collaboration, and adherence to best practices and regulations, ultimately contributing to the success of data-driven initiatives in today's complex business environment.

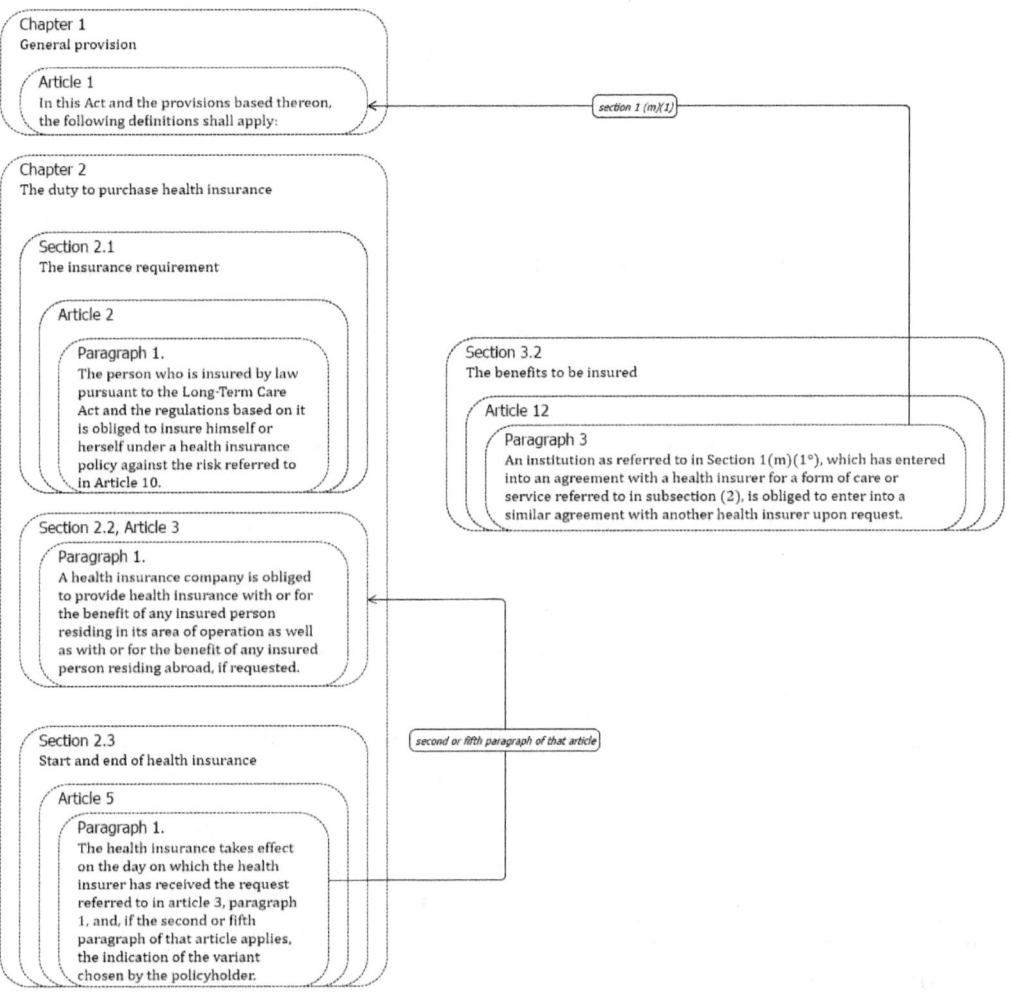

Figure 33: Legal articles with references.

10.5 Fact Expressions

In the quest to synchronize information across the enterprise, accuracy is paramount. Achieving this precision necessitates the rigorous verification of our models.

> *While visual aids like pictures and diagrams facilitate our understanding of the models, the formal verification process predominantly relies on written text. This text serves as the keystone for establishing the correctness of our models and is enriched by the indispensable words from the very heart of the business itself.*

The process of regenerating expressions, post-model creation, takes on a critical role in the verification journey. It encompasses the integration of essential components: examples, rules, verbalizations, and annotations, presented in an accessible and user-friendly format. By reinvigorating the models with these elements, we ensure that the models not only remain accurate, but also offer a comprehensive representation of real-world complexities. Through this process, we fortify the alignment of our information, thus enhancing the effectiveness and reliability of our enterprise-wide endeavors.

10.6 Examples

The essence of effective communication and information modeling lies in our ability to establish a common understanding of concepts, definitions, and data.

While naming things and crafting precise definitions are pivotal steps, including concrete examples truly solidifying our shared comprehension.

Examples serve as the bridge that connects theory to practicality. They are not merely illustrative but essential for verifying whether we are discussing the same entities and processes. By presenting tangible instances, we can affirm that our interpretations align, and our models accurately represent real-world scenarios.

Moreover, the inclusion of example populations goes beyond mere illustration. These populations may originate from diverse sources and states, representing a range of perspectives. They can be confirmed by business stakeholders to validate our models or provided as counterexamples, demonstrating what certain concepts are not. This approach not only sharpens the precision of our models, but also fosters transparency and alignment with business needs.

By emphasizing the role of examples, we ensure that our models are not merely theoretical constructs but practical solutions that truly reflect the complexities of the real world.

10.7 Rules

Fact-oriented modeling significantly emphasizes articulating and formalizing business rules within the information model. These rules serve as the bedrock upon which the model operates, governing the logic and behavior of the system. Business rules are encapsulated in fact-oriented modeling as declarative facts, making them clear, concise, and easy to understand. This clarity is vital as it ensures that all stakeholders, including business users and technical experts, have a common understanding of how the system operates and the constraints that govern it.

Business rules play a pivotal role in ensuring data integrity and consistency. They prevent data anomalies and inaccuracies by explicitly defining the conditions, constraints, and dependencies that guide data relationships. For instance, a business rule may dictate that, "A customer must have a unique customer ID," ensuring that duplicate customer entries are not permitted. In the context of fact-oriented modeling, these rules are not hidden in complex code but are explicitly stated as facts, making them easily accessible and enforceable.

Moreover, fact-oriented modeling allows for the agile evolution of business rules. As business requirements change, we can introduce or modify new texts to document these changes. This flexibility ensures that the information model remains adaptable and responsive to the evolving needs of the business, thus making it a potent tool for achieving both regulatory compliance and operational excellence.

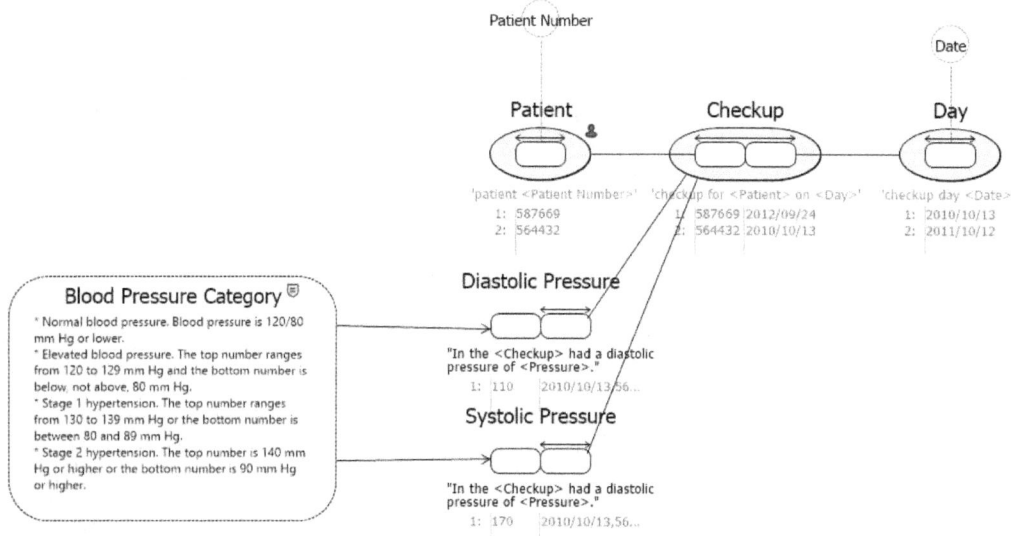

Figure 34: Business rule description with references.

10.8 Process

Fact-oriented modeling takes a dedicated approach to understanding and representing business processes, recognizing the critical role that a comprehensive understanding of data flow plays in designing effective information models. Unlike traditional approaches, FOM goes beyond treating business processes as abstract concepts, explicitly modeling them as a series of events that involve the creation and utilization of facts.

This modeling approach provides a structured and precise foundation to support business processes. Each step within a process is intricately linked to the facts necessary for data administration. These facts create a clear and visual representation of the information needs associated with the business process. Stakeholders, therefore, gain a shared understanding of the process dynamics and how data interacts within it, fostering effective collaboration.

Figure 35 illustrates an Activity Diagram with Facts, showcasing the integration of fact-oriented modeling into the depiction of business processes. This visual representation enhances the clarity and accessibility of the information model.

In essence, fact-oriented modeling places business processes at the forefront of the information model. It ensures that the model isn't merely a static representation of data but a dynamic reflection of how data is created, processed, and utilized in the real world. This dynamic perspective significantly enhances the model's utility and relevance for organizations seeking to optimize their operations and master their data management challenges. Fact-oriented modeling, with its emphasis on facts, aligns business processes and information models to foster organizational efficiency and effectiveness.

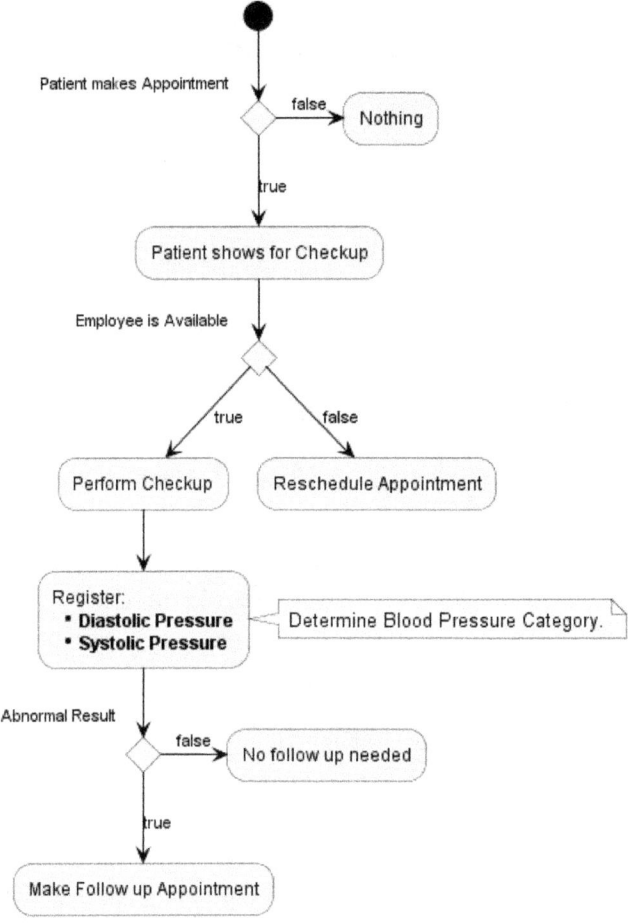

Figure 35: Activity diagram with facts.

10.9 Events

A relatively new kid on the block is the so-called data event. Applications handle data and store it in a database, but the actions themselves can also be logged or streamed into a logging environment. Logging events when they happen and the data registered with them allows flexible infrastructures. It is especially helpful for streaming, and building timelines after a process has occurred.

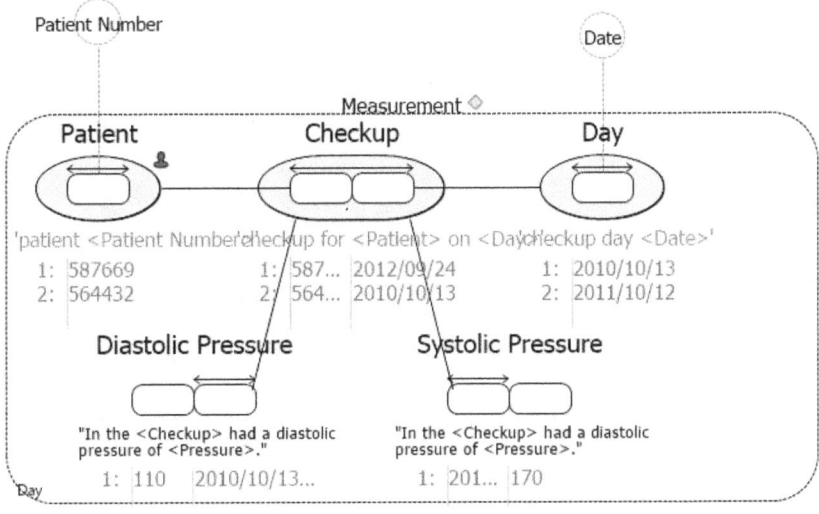

Figure 36: Events involving various elements.

A measurement, in this case, can be modeled as an event. It should then include patient, day, and blood pressure measures. By grouping the information elements needed, we can name and visualize these in the existing model, ensuring we align with the business information.

SECTION FOUR

Data Modelers and Engineers

This section is for the data modelers and engineers who are the backbone of technology implementation. It dives deep into the intricate world of data and how to transform raw data into valuable information, insights, and applications.

11. Model Transformation

In the transformation phase of the fact-oriented modeling approach, CaseTalk applies a series of generic steps to prepare the model for generating artifacts. These steps involve altering the fact-oriented model to make it more suitable for the generators. The three main steps in the transformation process are Group, Lexicalize, and Reduce.

11.1 Grouping

In the Group step, we can remove fact types containing roles with an identical population elsewhere, as determined by constraints. This helps simplify the model by eliminating redundant information. However, to maintain the correctness of the information, other roles may need to be moved elsewhere to ensure the relationships are still properly represented.

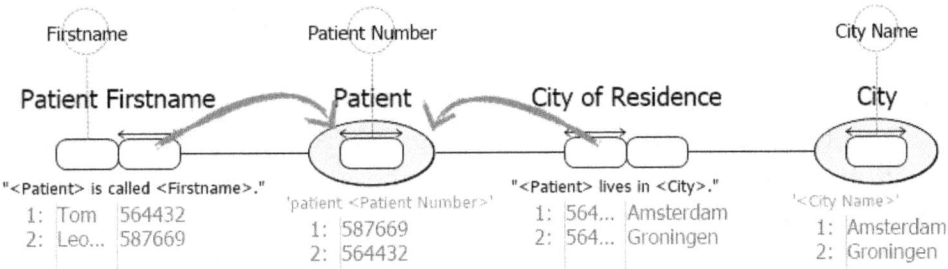

Figure 37: Model transformation – Before Grouping.

11.2 Lexicalizing

The Lexicalize step ensures that all roles are played by a label type in the information model. This involves resolving all substitutions through object types until the final label types are reached. Once this transformation is complete, no object types will be left in the information model, only fact types and label types. This step helps establish a clear and consistent vocabulary for the model.

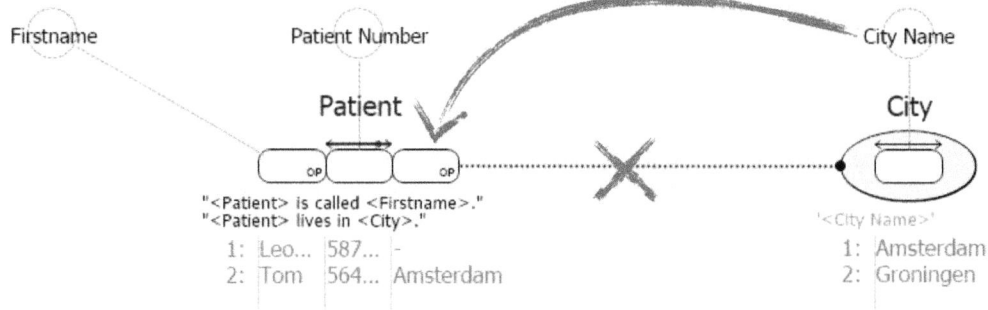

Figure 38: Model transformation - Lexicalizing.

11.3 Reducing

In the Reduce step, we remove object types that no longer add value to the model. This typically occurs after the Group and Lexicalize steps, as redundant information is already eliminated. Removing these redundant object types helps streamline the model and improves its clarity and efficiency. The last step removed the object type for City since all communication and tuples will exist under the Fact type Patient.

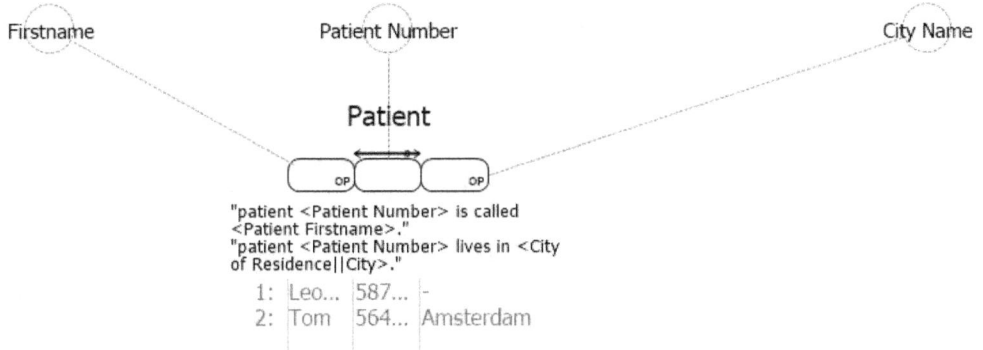

Figure 39: Model transformation - After Reducing.

By applying these transformation steps, CaseTalk ensures that the fact-oriented model is optimized for generating artifacts. This allows IT staff to derive useful deliverables from the model that align with the requirements and accurately reflect the language and structure of the domain.

11.4 Only Lexicalization

We've mentioned and shown the relational models (see Paragraph 9.2) that happen after grouping, reducing, and lexicalizing. We've also mentioned UML Class Diagrams (see Paragraph 9.3), which only require Grouping. But we want to show you the capabilities of deploying only lexicalization. The result is a class of its own, called the **Column Store.** With a simple choice of transformation steps, the information models can be transformed into a wide variety of data structures. Only performing lexicalization would create a database like a column store. It allows flexible schema management but may require lots of business rules to manage, and joins to represent the information. A column store is almost identical to a table per fact type.

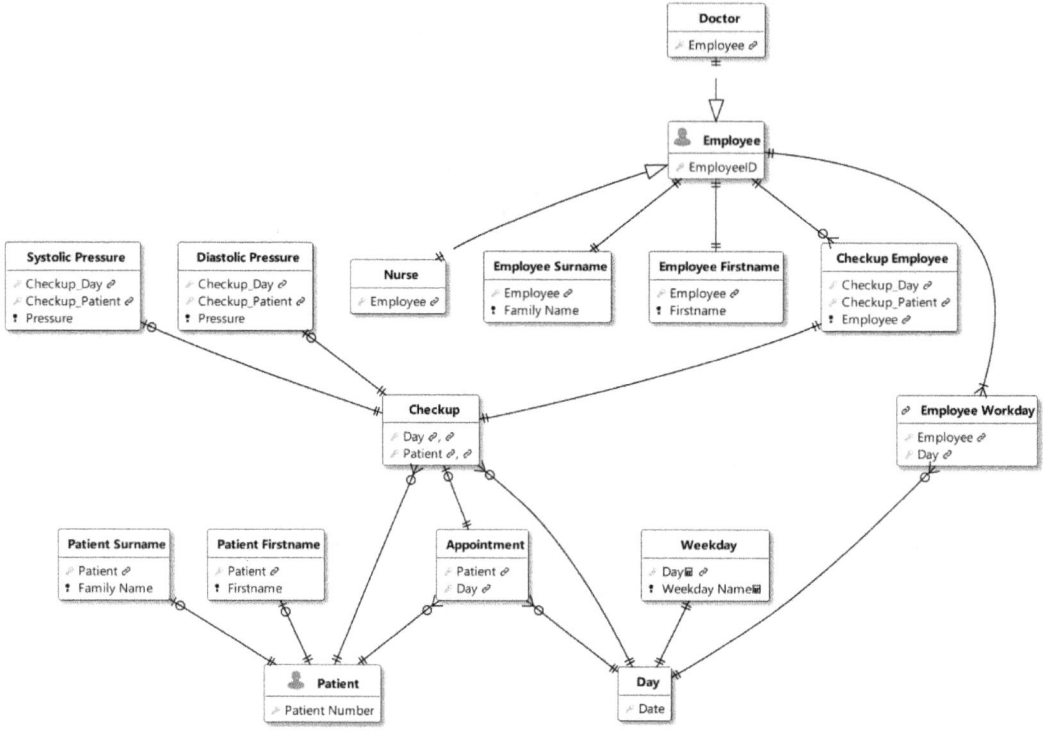

Figure 40: Lexicalizing to column store.

11.5 Rules Drive the logical model

We use the constraints in the information model to drive the model-to-model transformation. The following examples play with mandatory and uniqueness constraints to demonstrate the effect of foreign keys in the logical model.

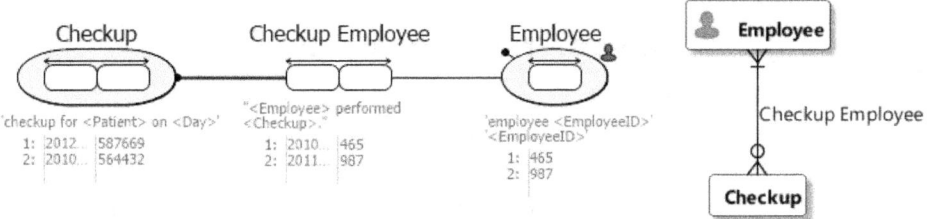

Figure 41: Checkup Employee with a wide unicity constraint.

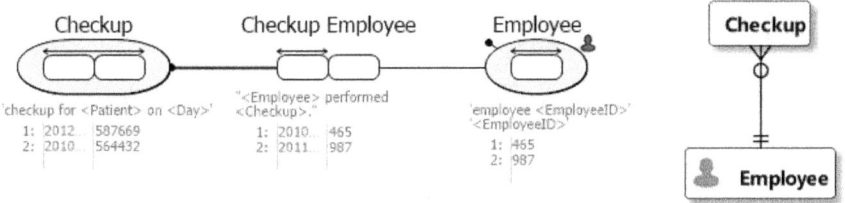

Figure 42: Checkup Employee with a unicity constraint on checkup.

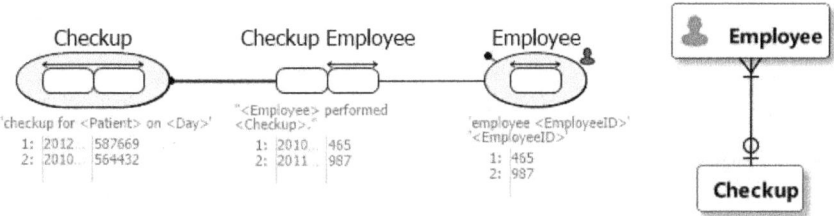

Figure 43: Checkup Employee with a unicity constraint on Employee.

The information model and its business constraints completely drive the foreign keys from the logical diagram and the cardinalities. The same goes for facts to become a table of their own or simply an attribute in another. All is driven by the constraints.

11.6 Ensemble Logical model

The Ensemble Logical Model is a set of artifacts to document high-level concepts, attributes, and relations. You can import these to start building your information model.

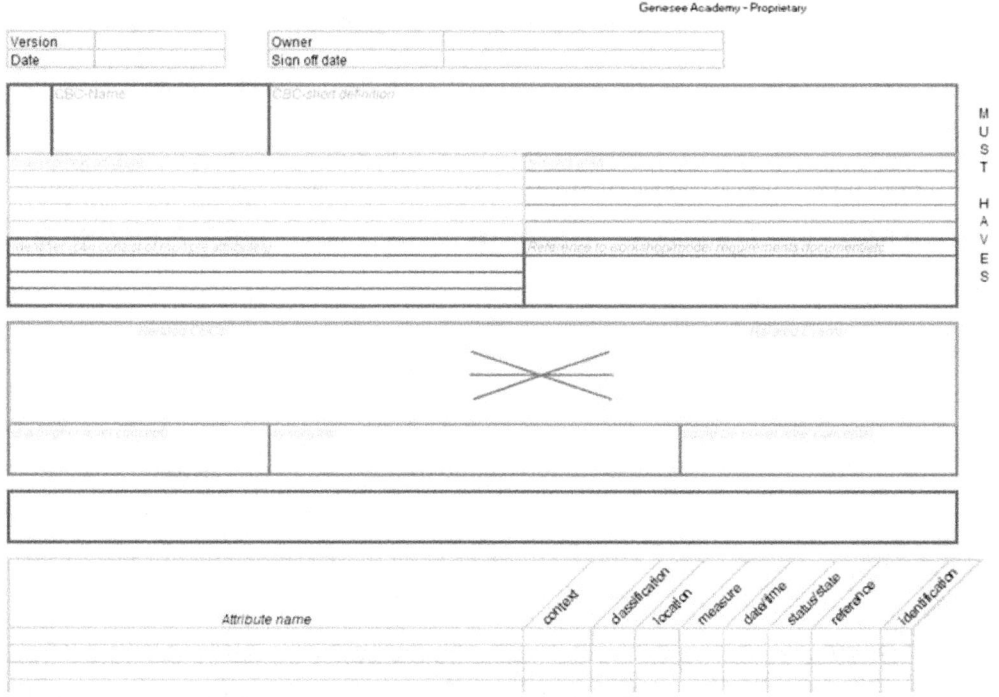

Figure 44: Ensemble logical modeling artifact.

The artifact input is an easy method to finally come to a technical implementation into any Ensemble Modeling pattern, such as Data Vault, Anchor Modeling, and Focal Point. At the core, these patterns all attempt to find the business concepts that are part of the data warehouse solution.

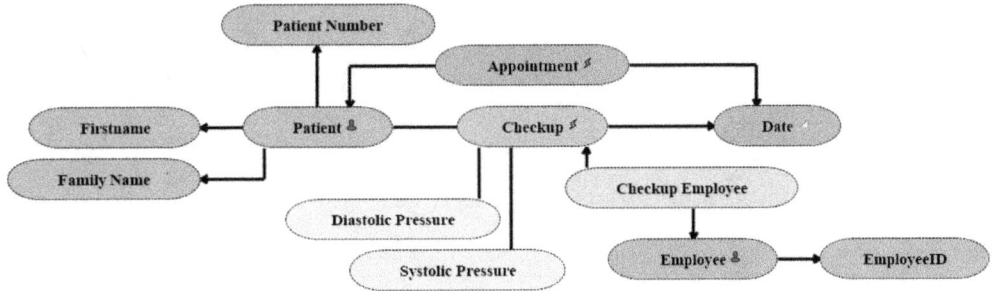

Figure 45: Imported ensemble logical modeling artifact.

Once those are imported, we can add fact expressions, examples, and constraints to promote the concepts to a solid verifiable information model.

As an illustration of how information modeling is a natural fit, the hubs are business concepts (Patient and Day), satellites for the contextual data (Firstname, Surname, and WeekDay), and links (Checkup) for the relationships between the concepts.

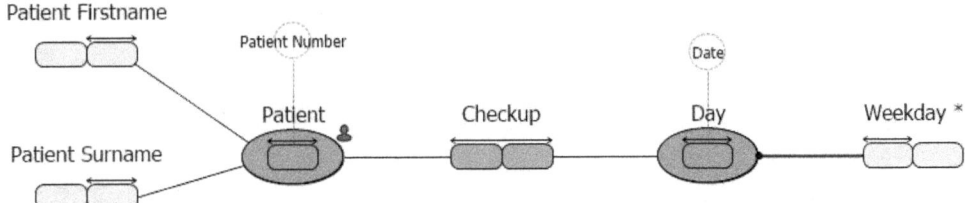

Figure 46: Data Vault recognizes hubs, satellites, and links.

Artifacts for Data Vault implementations can now be automatically generated, including timelines, source lineage, etc.

12. Artifacts

Having meticulously gathered and structured the facts within our information model, the natural progression is to transform this knowledge into tangible artifacts readily deployable to IT professionals. CaseTalk proves to be an invaluable companion in this endeavor, offering an array of generators capable of producing diverse outputs based on the meticulously crafted fact-oriented model.

Within the toolkit of CaseTalk, a comprehensive suite of generators is at your disposal, each serving a distinct purpose. These generators harness the power of the fact-oriented model, effectively translating it into practical resources for IT system development. Some of the notable generators within the CaseTalk ecosystem include:

12.1 Business Glossary

In addition to generating artifacts for IT system implementation, CaseTalk can create business-oriented information reports. These reports bridge technical and business domains, providing clear and concise documentation that enhances understanding and collaboration. Moreover, these reports can be seamlessly integrated into the information model, serving a dual purpose.

These business reports are invaluable for non-technical stakeholders, enabling them to grasp the information model's concepts, definitions, and annotations without diving into the technical intricacies. They serve as a valuable resource for business users, enabling effective communication and fostering a shared understanding of critical concepts.

Furthermore, the ability to merge these reports back into the information model is a testament to CaseTalk's flexibility. It allows for the continuous refinement and expansion of the information model, reflecting new definitions and annotations that evolve in response to changing business needs and requirements. This dynamic process ensures that the model remains a living entity that adapts to the evolving landscape of the organization, maintaining its relevance and accuracy over time.

12.2 Mapping for Lineage and Governance

CaseTalk introduces a robust set of capabilities for mapping metadata from both offline and live catalogs to the conceptual information model in the ever-evolving landscape of data governance and lineage tracking sources. This integration enhances the transparency and traceability of data and fortifies data governance and lineage practices.

Catalogs, often housing a wealth of valuable metadata, can be seamlessly integrated with the conceptual information model, providing a comprehensive understanding of data assets. This mapping process unearths the relationships between data elements, making it evident how data flows through the organization's ecosystem. By bridging the gap between conceptual models and metadata, it becomes easier to visualize the journey of data.

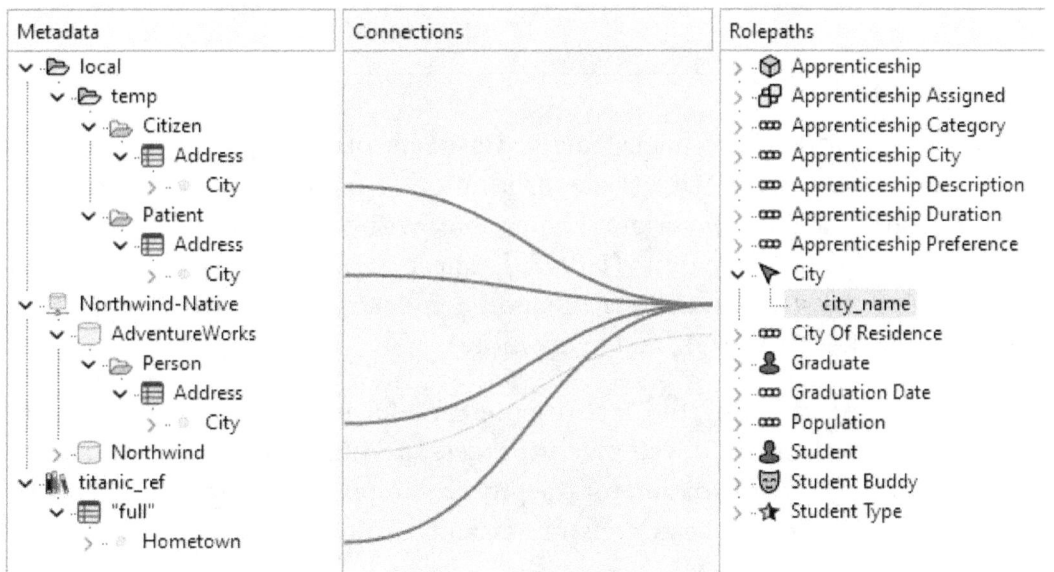

Figure 47: Source system to information model mapping.

CaseTalk's support for live catalogs further elevates the capabilities for lineage and governance. Real-time access to metadata catalogs ensures that the information model remains synchronized with the dynamic data landscape. This live connection empowers organizations to maintain an accurate and up-to-date understanding of data sources, transformations, and destinations, strengthening data governance practices.

In essence, CaseTalk's metadata mapping capabilities create a unified ecosystem where conceptual information models, offline catalogs, and live data sources work in harmony. This harmonious collaboration not only promotes enhanced data lineage and governance, but also fosters a holistic understanding of data assets, laying the foundation for more informed decision-making and regulatory compliance.

12.3 Relational Databases

In the realm of database management, CaseTalk offers a powerful feature to speed up generating DDL (Data Definition Language) and DML (Data Manipulation Language) scripts compatible with a spectrum of relational database management systems (DBMSs). These SQL scripts meet the specific requirements of various DBMSs, including industry giants like Oracle, SQL Server, MySQL, PostgreSQL, and many more.

By seamlessly converting the fact-oriented model into SQL scripts, CaseTalk streamlines the database development process, saving valuable time and effort. These scripts lay the foundation for the physical implementation of the database, defining tables, columns, keys, constraints, and relationships, in accordance with the intricacies of each DBMS.

This versatility in script generation is a testament to CaseTalk's adaptability, ensuring that organizations can effortlessly deploy their information models across diverse database platforms. Whether it's creating, altering, or querying data, CaseTalk's SQL script generation capabilities pave the way for efficient database design, offering a dynamic solution that caters to the unique needs of each DBMS.

```
CREATE DOMAIN Blood_Pressure_Type AS CHAR(9)
  CHECK (VALUE IN ('diastolic', 'systolic', 'normal'));
CREATE DOMAIN Patient_Number AS INTEGER;
CREATE DOMAIN Pressure AS CHAR(7);
/*

In the checkup on <DateTime_Date> at <DateTime_Time>, the
    patient <Patient> had a diastolic pressure of
    <Diastolic Pressure>.

In the checkup on <DateTime_Date> at <DateTime_Time>, the
    patient <Patient> had a systolic pressure of
    <Systolic Pressure>.

The checkup on <DateTime_Date> at <DateTime_Time>, the
    patient <Patient> shows signs of <Checkup_Result>.

*/
CREATE TABLE Patient_Checkup (
  DateTime_Date Date NOT NULL,
  DateTime_Time Time NOT NULL,
  Patient Patient_Number NOT NULL,
  Diastolic_Pressure Pressure,
  Systolic_Pressure Pressure,
  Checkup_Result Blood_Pressure_Type,
  PRIMARY KEY (DateTime_Date, DateTime_Time, Patient)

);
```

Figure 48: Generated SQL DDL.

Since the information model already contains examples, we may also load an initial population into the database for initial development and testing.

```
INSERT INTO Patient_Checkup
```

```
    (DateTime_Date, DateTime_Time, Patient,
      Diastolic_Pressure, Systolic_Pressure)
VALUES
    ('12-10-2019', '14:00:00', 123499, '170mmHg', '110mmHg');

ALTER TABLE Patient_Checkup
  ADD FOREIGN KEY (Patient)
  REFERENCES Patient (Patient_Number);
```

Figure 49: Generated SQL DML.

And those scripts also generate database views, which can be considered pre-made queries. Some of the views which can be generated bring verbalizations of facts back to the application developers, and their users. The users are quite commonly the domain experts who provided the fact verbalizations in the first place.

```
CREATE VIEW Patient_Checkup_Expression AS
  SELECT
     DateTime_Date, DateTime_Time, Patient,
     'In the checkup on ' || cast(DateTime_Date as varchar) ||
     ' at ' || cast(DateTime_Time as varchar) ||
     ', the patient ' || cast(Patient as varchar) ||
     ' had a diastolic pressure of ' ||
     cast(Diastolic_Pressure as varchar) || '.' AS Fact
  FROM Patient_Checkup

  UNION
  SELECT
     DateTime_Date, DateTime_Time, Patient,
     'In the checkup on ' || cast(DateTime_Date as varchar) ||
     ' at ' || cast(DateTime_Time as varchar) ||
     ', the patient ' || cast(Patient as varchar) ||
     ' had a systolic pressure of ' ||
     cast(Systolic_Pressure as varchar) || '.' AS Fact
  FROM Patient_Checkup;
```

Figure 50: Generated SQL expression layer.

12.4 Messages, Data Events, Documents

In the domain of data exchange and communication, CaseTalk extends its capabilities to generate XML and JSON Schemas tailored for messaging and web server environments. These schemas play a pivotal role in defining the structure, format, and validation rules for data events, messages, and documents.

For organizations engaged in data exchange, XML and JSON schemas are instrumental for ensuring data consistency, integrity, and compatibility across various systems and platforms. CaseTalk's schema generation feature simplifies this process by automatically converting the fact-oriented model into XML and JSON schemas, optimized for messaging and web server environments.

```
     <xs:complexType name="Checkup">
  <xs:annotation>
    <xs:documentation xml:lang="en">
<![CDATA[[Expressions]

"In the checkup for <Patient> on <Day> had a diastolic
    pressure of <Diastolic Pressure>."

"In the checkup for <Patient> on <Day> had a diastolic
    pressure of <Systolic Pressure>."

"<Checkup Employee> performed checkup for <Patient> on <Day>."

  ]]>
    </xs:documentation>
  </xs:annotation>
  <xs:sequence>
    <xs:element name="Diastolic_Pressure" type="Pressure"
        minOccurs="0" maxOccurs="1" />
    <xs:element name="Day" type="Day" />
    <xs:element name="Patient" type="Patient" />
```

```
      <xs:element name="Systolic_Pressure" type="Pressure"
            minOccurs="0" maxOccurs="1" />
      <xs:element name="Checkup_Employee" type="Employee" />
   </xs:sequence>
</xs:complexType>
```

Figure 51: Generated XSD snippet.

This functionality offers a dual advantage. Firstly, it streamlines the creation of data structures that adhere to industry standards, facilitating seamless data exchange and interoperability. Secondly, it ensures that the generated schemas align with the specific requirements of messaging systems and web servers, thus promoting data transmission and reception efficiency.

```
{
"name": "Checkup",
"description":
  "In the checkup for patient <Patient> on checkup day <Day>
      had a diastolic pressure of <Diastolic Pressure>.
    In the checkup
for patient <Patient> on checkup day <Day>
      had a diastolic pressure of <Systolic Pressure>.
    Employee <Employee> performed checkup
for patient <Patient>
      on checkup day <Day>.",
"schema": {
   "fields": [
     {
       "name": "Day",
       "title": "Day/Date",
       "type": "string",
       "constraints": {
         "required": "true",
         "maxLength": "10"
       }
     },
     {
       "name": "Patient",
       "title": "Patient/Patient Number",
```

```
        "type": "integer",
        "constraints": {
          "required": "true"
        }
      },
      {
        "name": "Diastolic_Pressure",
        "title": "Diastolic Pressure",
        "type": "string"
      },
      {
        "name": "Systolic_Pressure",
        "title": "Systolic Pressure",
        "type": "string"
      }
    ],
    "primaryKey": [
      "Day", "Patient"
    ],
    "foreignKeys": [
      {
        "fields": [
          "Day", "Patient"
        ],
        "reference": {
          "resource": "Appointment",
          "fields": [
            "Day", "Patient"
          ]
        }
      }
    ]
  }
}
```

Figure 52: Generated JSON snippet.

By enabling organizations to effortlessly create XML and JSON schemas from their fact-oriented models, CaseTalk enhances the clarity, accuracy, and efficiency of data exchange, contributing to the success of data-driven initiatives in the modern digital landscape.

12.5 Semantic Web and Knowledge Graph

In the era of the Semantic Web, CaseTalk embraces the concept of knowledge representation through the generation of OWL (Web Ontology Language) and RDF (Resource Description Framework) formats. These formats are optimized for semantic web environments, offering a structured and standardized way to represent and exchange knowledge on the web.

OWL and RDF are essential tools for organizations looking to participate in the emerging field of the Semantic Web. CaseTalk simplifies creating OWL ontologies and RDF data, ensuring that the fact-oriented model is effectively translated into these formats. By doing so, organizations can contribute to developing a more interconnected and intelligent web, where data is not just data but also a source of knowledge.

These are crafted in a technical environment and lack a consistent, repeatable process to model business using a method. The result is hard for domain experts to verify. On the other hand, once an information model is built and verified, an OWL/RDF file can be easily generated from it.

```
<owl:Class rdf:about="#Checkup">
  <skos:prefLabel xml:lang="en-US">Checkup</skos:prefLabel>
  <rdfs:subClassOf>
    <owl:Class>
      <owl:intersectionOf rdf:parseType="Collection">
        <owl:Restriction>
          <owl:onProperty rdf:resource="#CheckupEmployee" />
          <!-- Checkup Employee -->
          <owl:minCardinality>1</owl:minCardinality>
        </owl:Restriction>
```

```
        <owl:Restriction>
          <owl:onProperty rdf:resource="#CheckupEmployee" />
          <owl:maxCardinality>1</owl:maxCardinality>
        </owl:Restriction>
      </owl:intersectionOf>
    </owl:Class>
  </rdfs:subClassOf>
</owl:Class>
```

Figure 53: Generated RDF/OWL snippet.

12.6 System Development

Source Code. System development is a dynamic and multifaceted process that requires efficient tools and resources to translate concepts and models into functioning IT systems. CaseTalk offers support for a range of programming languages and systems, ensuring that the development journey is seamless and optimized for various environments.

Application developers create applications for the business and need to somehow align with business terminology. There are various approaches to accomplish that. There's Domain Driven Design, Domain Specific Languages, Event Storming—all different approaches and techniques to allow developers to get as close to the business concepts and terminology as possible.

It doesn't matter which language the developers use; they are all challenged by similar issues. Once we build an information model, generating the initial code is as easy as pressing a button.

Python has become a powerhouse in the world of software development, and CaseTalk ensures that Python developers have access to source code snippets that expedite the system development process. These Python code segments are generated based on the fact-oriented model, promoting efficiency and reliability in Python-based projects.

```python
class Checkup(CaseTalkBaseClass):
  """
    <Checkup> is unique on <Day> and <Patient>.
  """
  diastolic_pressure: str = field(
    metadata={
      'name':
        'Diastolic Pressure'})
  day: Day = field(
    metadata={
      'required': True,
        'key': True,
        'name': 'Day'})
  patient: Patient = field(
    metadata={
      'required': True,
        'key': True,
        'name': 'Patient'})
  systolic_pressure: str = field(
    metadata={
      'name': 'Systolic Pressure'})
  employee: Employee = field(
    metadata={
      'required': True,
      'name': 'Checkup Employee'})
  @staticmethod
  def express(): return f"""\
    "In the checkup for {patient} on {day} had a diastolic"\
    "pressure of {diastolic_Pressure}.\n"\
    "In the checkup for {patient} on {day} had a systolic"\
    "pressure of {systolic_Pressure}.\n"\
    "{employee} performed checkup for {patient} on {day}."
```

Figure 54: Generated Python snippet.

Natural Language Processing. The world of natural language processing and text analysis benefits from CaseTalk's support for spaCy. It allows for generating spaCy-compatible code snippets that are in harmony with the fact-oriented model. This feature enhances the development of advanced text processing and analysis systems.

```
nlp = spacy.blank("en")
  training_data = [
    ("Utrecht", [
        (0, 7, "City Name")
        ]),
    ("New York", [
        (0, 8, "City Name")
        ]),
    ("Portland", [
        (0, 8, "City Name")
        ]),
    ("Nurse 465", [
       (6, 3, "EmployeeID"),
       (6, 3, "Employee")
       ]),
    ("Doctor 987", [
       (7, 3, "EmployeeID"),
       (7, 3, "Employee")
       ]),
    ("Patient 564432 is called Tom.", [
       (0, 14, "Patient Number"),
       (0, 14, "Patient"),
       (0, 14, "Person"),
       (37, 3, "Firstname"),
       ])
```

Figure 55: Generated spaCy snippet.

Database Design Tools. In the domain of database design, CaseTalk offers a diverse range of capabilities to facilitate the creation and management of database structures. These features cater to various database design tools and data export formats, ensuring the seamless translation of conceptual models into practical databases.

CaseTalk allows for the generation of Visual Basic scripts to employ in a variety of database design tools, including Microsoft Access, PowerDesigner, **and** ER/Studio. These scripts streamline transforming the fact-oriented model into a database schema, optimizing the database design and development process.

12.7 Artificial Intelligence

Even though AI is based on theories and practices a few decades old, the current pace of generative AI seems to outrun any hype currently on the market. The benefits of this technology are off the charts, and we probably haven't seen anything yet.

The one thing most experts seem to agree upon now is that good data is required to train the AI properly. And applying AI without that is simply betting on a magical potion. As many books on AI, Bias, and Absent Data have illustrated, to be sure, you need a solid and complete picture first.

However, it does not prevent AI from being applied as an assistant or even a trainee. The hallucination aspects can help us start asking questions about the data and get answers from the business domain experts, who hopefully will tell us, "No, that's not how it works."

And why are we hoping for a negative instead of finding the hallucinated confirmations, you may ask? Whenever we assume a statement or a fact, we introduce our own bias. Whenever the experts tell us the matter is different than we assumed, we have learned something and, simultaneously, removed our own bias. This is why information modeling is crucial in every aspect of data.

AI Prompt

Sending our fact expressions with the following prompt "Based on the following classified fact expressions, please provide a business case description. In addition to this case, please provide questions for further investigation." to ChatGPT, its response can provide some insight and further help:

AI Response

Business Case Description:

This business case involves the appointments, blood pressure, checkup employees, city of residence, diastolic pressure, employee firstname, employee surname, employee workday, patient firstname, patient surname, systolic pressure, and weekday of two patients, Tom Harvey and Leonard Reed. Tom Harvey has an appointment for checkup day 2010/10/13 and Leonard Reed has an appointment for checkup day 2012/09/24. In the checkup for each patient, they had a blood pressure type and pressure. Employee 465, Jack Johnson, performed checkup for Tom Harvey on checkup day 2010/10/13 and 2011/10/12, and Employee 987, Mary Jackson, performed checkup for Leonard Reed on checkup day 2011/09/09. Tom Harvey lives in New York and Leonard Reed lives in Portland. In the checkup for each patient they had a diastolic pressure and systolic pressure. Checkup day 2010/10/13 was a Wednesday and checkup day 2012/09/24 was a Monday.

Questions for Further Investigation:

- What is the blood pressure type and pressure of each patient?
- What is the diastolic pressure and systolic pressure of each patient?
- What other checkups did Employees 465 and 987 perform on checkup day 2010/10/13 and 2011/10/12?
- What other appointments did Tom Harvey and Leonard Reed have?
- Are there any other patients that live in New York and Portland?

13. Appendix

13.1 Patient Record

Simple examples may lower your sense of value for FCO-IM; therefore, we need to show you the real power of the method by advancing to more complicated topics.

Fact expression can be modeled in different manners without losing meaning to the domain expert. These variations are semantically equivalent. Take, for example, the following expressions, which only differ in underlining:

"At <u>the checkup of patient 12345 on 2010/01/01</u> had a systolic pressure is <u>170mmHg</u>."

"At <u>the checkup of patient 12345 on 2010/01/01</u> had a <u>systolic</u> pressure is <u>170mmHg</u>."

We will show two different structures of modeling, as shown in Figure 56.

The decision to model systolic/diastolic pressure as two fact types is a choice determined by the business. Abstraction can be a technical choice, but the business should be leading. Therefore, it is important to keep asking questions to domain experts. If the pressure has only two types of pressure, and both need to exist in parallel, it may make sense to choose the top structure. The bottom structure may be needed if the future is uncertain and the domain expert explains various pressure types to be captured. However, the fact expression itself is semantically equivalent and read identically.

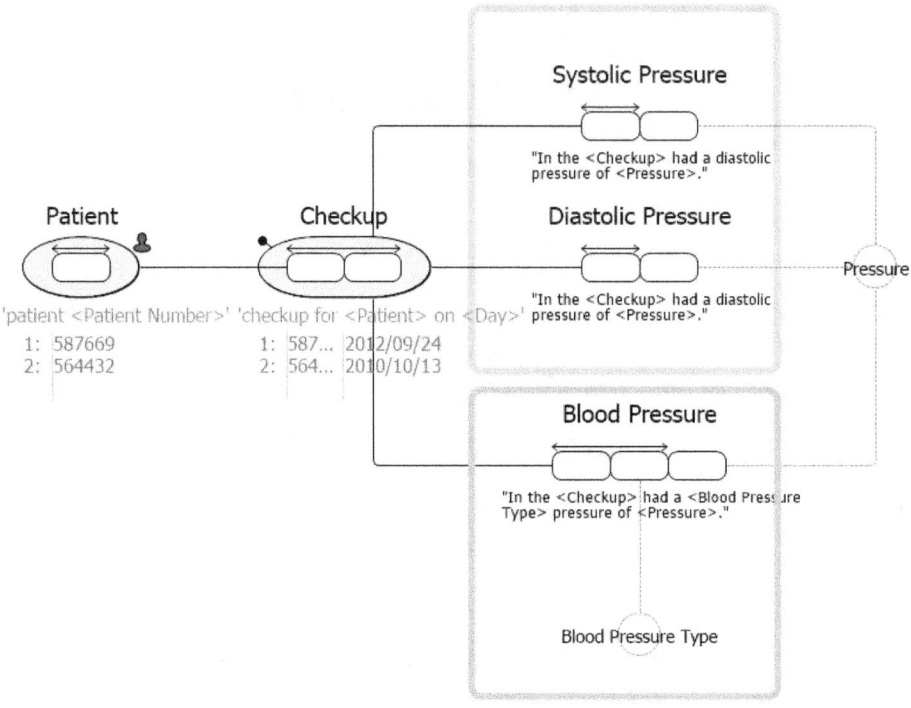

Figure 56: Identical facts, different structure.

13.2 We are all People

Different identifications may exist for the same object type. There are various ways to model that. However, the most common and more complicated option is to model them as generalized object types. The reason for that becomes apparent if that generalized object type has related fact types for all identifications.

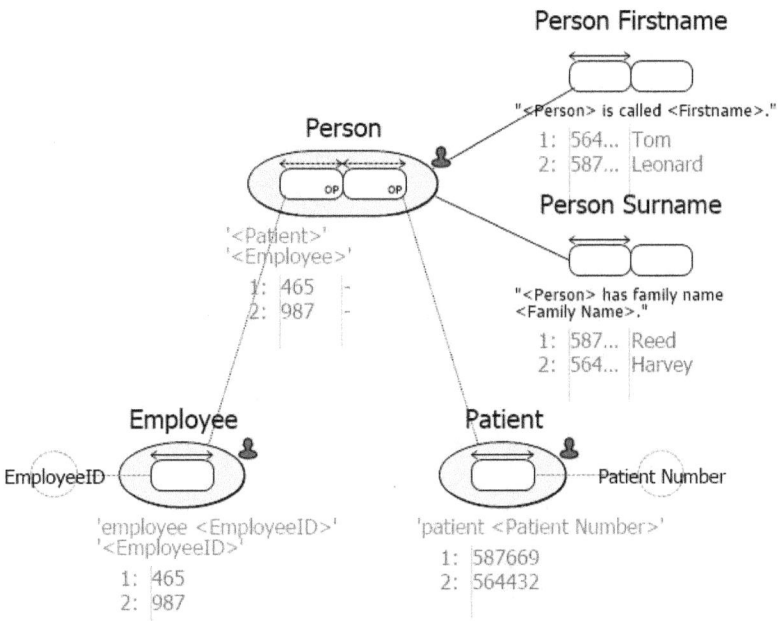

Figure 57: Generalized objects can be multiple things.

In Figure 57, the persons are modeled where they can have different identification structures. This can happen, for instance, when introducing the infamous object type Party. A party can be either a person or an organization; both are identified differently. A party can be modeled like a generalized object type using concrete facts like the person above.

13.3 Files and Folders

FCO-IM can capture recursive structures in information without problems. As an example, we will verbalize the file path, which contains folders and subfolders, a recursive structure:

```
"File C:\My Documents\Customers\John Doe\Contact.doc exists."
```

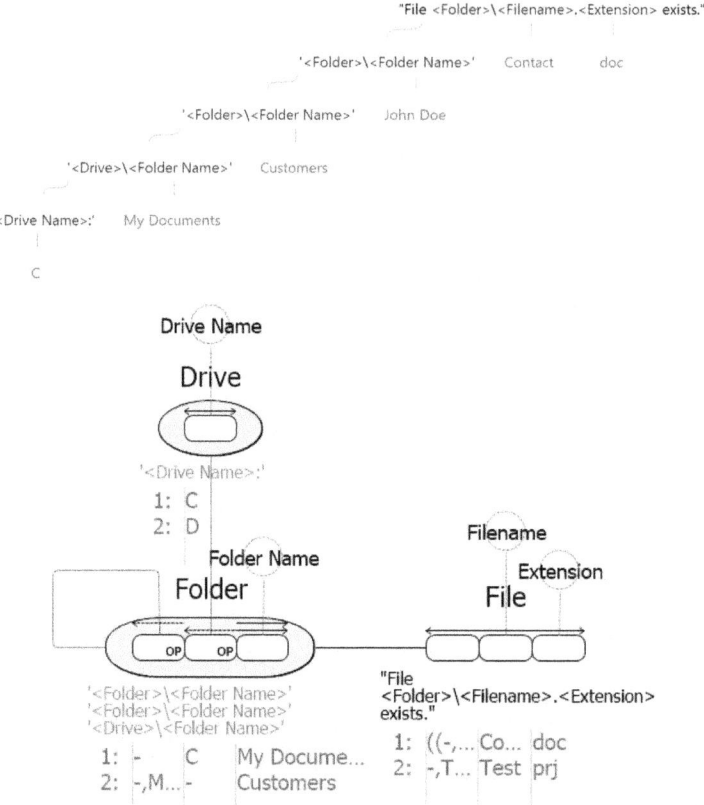

Figure 58: Recursive information structure.

Implementing this in a relational database is challenging without artificial keys and parent-child relationships. However, software effortlessly handles it, as it doesn't demand primary keys, relying instead on instance pointers in memory.

13.4 Business Process

This example shows how to model a business process. We write down the entire process as a scenario of facts.

APPENDIX • 131

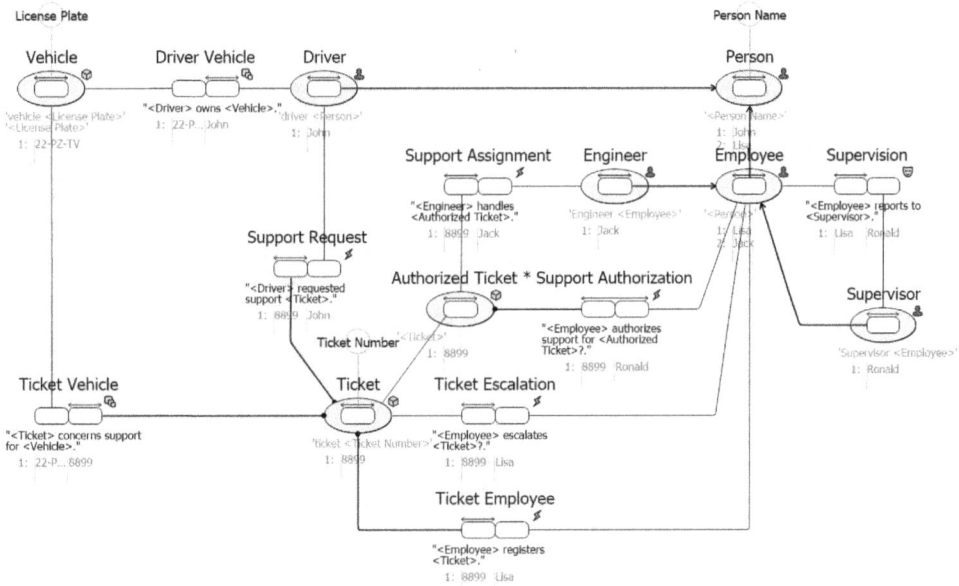

Figure 59: Support Request Information Model.

132 • INFORMATION MODELING

The various fact expressions show the relevant states of information. It uses a request, authorization, and escalation case. Different facts come to life in that case while the process is in motion. These facts are the basis for the information model, providing functionality for the system to support processes as available through facts. And the corresponding UML Class Diagram for developers:

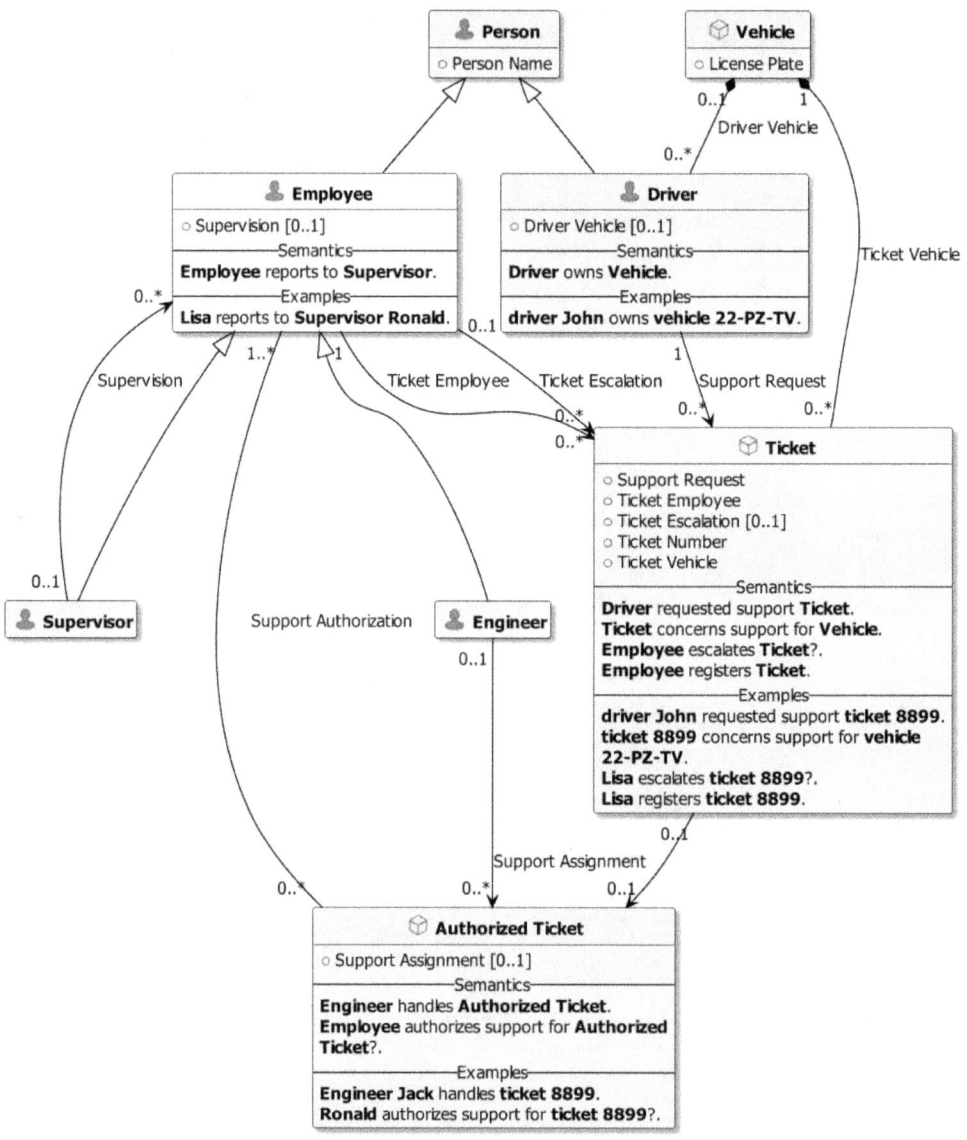

Figure 60: Support Request UML Diagram.

13.5 Decision Table

Every employee is entitled to at least 22 vacation days. Only employees, younger than 18 or at most 60, or employees with at least 30 employment years can receive 5 days extra. If the employee has 15 to 30 years of employment, 2 extra days are earned. Also employees older then 45 get 2 days extra. These 2 days cannot be combined with the previous additional 5 days. Employees older than 60 and employees having more than 30 years of employment get 3 days extra on top of the other extra days. We can create an overview of all conditions and outcomes in a so-called decision table.

Age	<18			18..45			45..60			>=60		
Employment Years	<15	15..30	>=30	<15	15..30	>=30	<15	15..30	>=30	<15	15..30	>=30
22 vacation days	x	x	x	x	x	x	x	x	x	x	x	x
5 extra days	x	x	x	-	-	x	-	-	x	x	x	x
2 extra days	-	-	-	-	x	-	x	x	-	-	-	-
3 extra days	-	-	-	-	-	x	-	-	x	x	x	x

Figure 61: Decision table.

Once we have the overview above, we can simplify the table to reduce the redundant outcomes for multiple conditions.

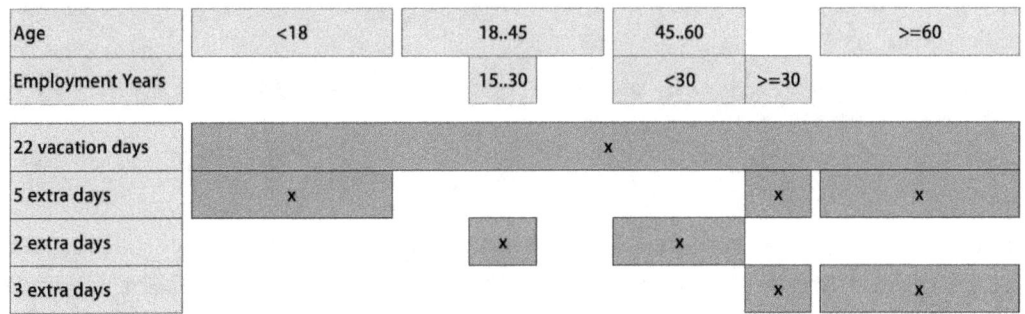

Figure 62: Reduced decision table.

134 • INFORMATION MODELING

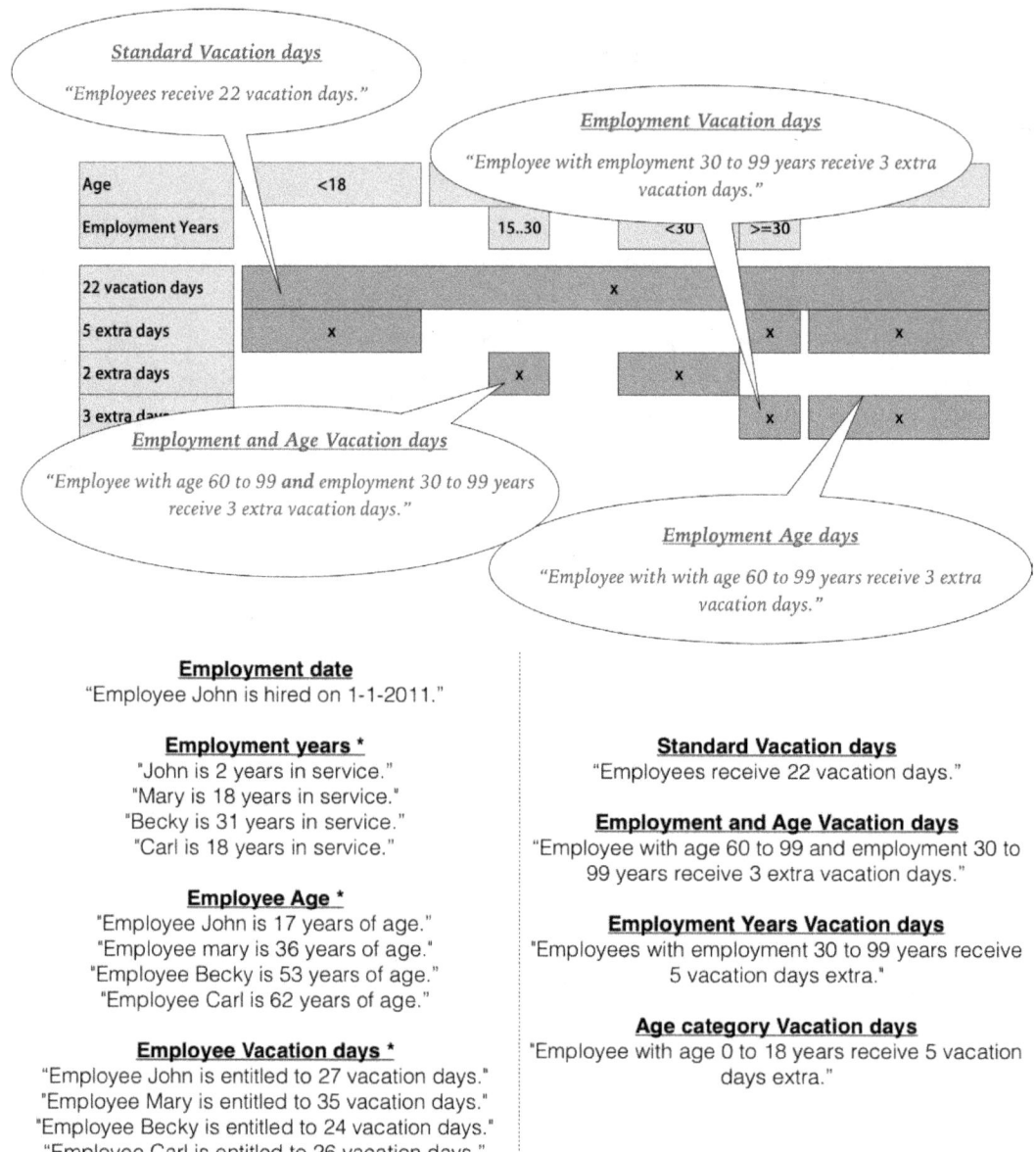

Figure 63: Verbalized Decision Table.

Figure 63 illustrates the verbalization of all possible outcomes, all xs. The verbalizations are accompanied by facts from the HR department to verify calculated outcomes for various employees.

APPENDIX • 135

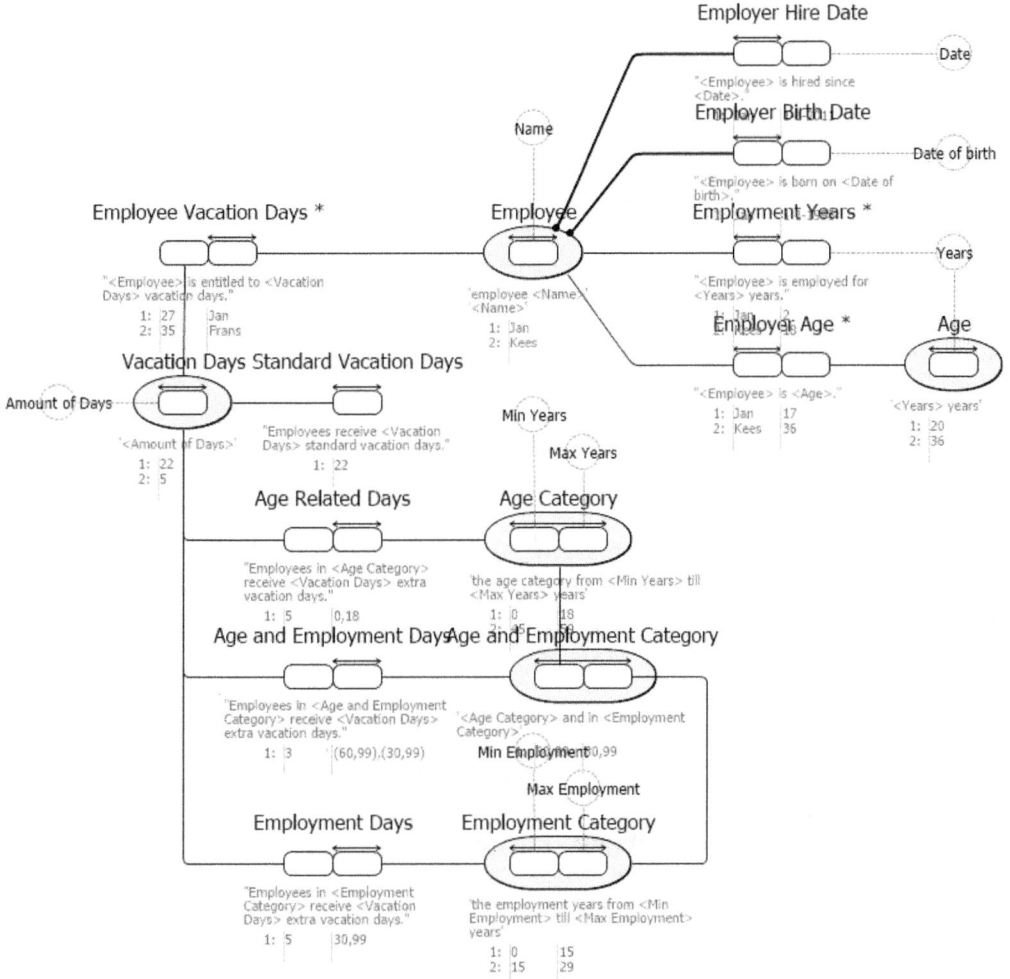

Figure 64: Modeled Decision Table.

The information model diagram renders both the parts reflecting the decision table as the facts from the HR department. The total number of vacation days an employee receives is captured in the fact type Employee Vacation Days, which is the sum of entitled vacation days. This calculated fact is indicated by the "*" next to its name.

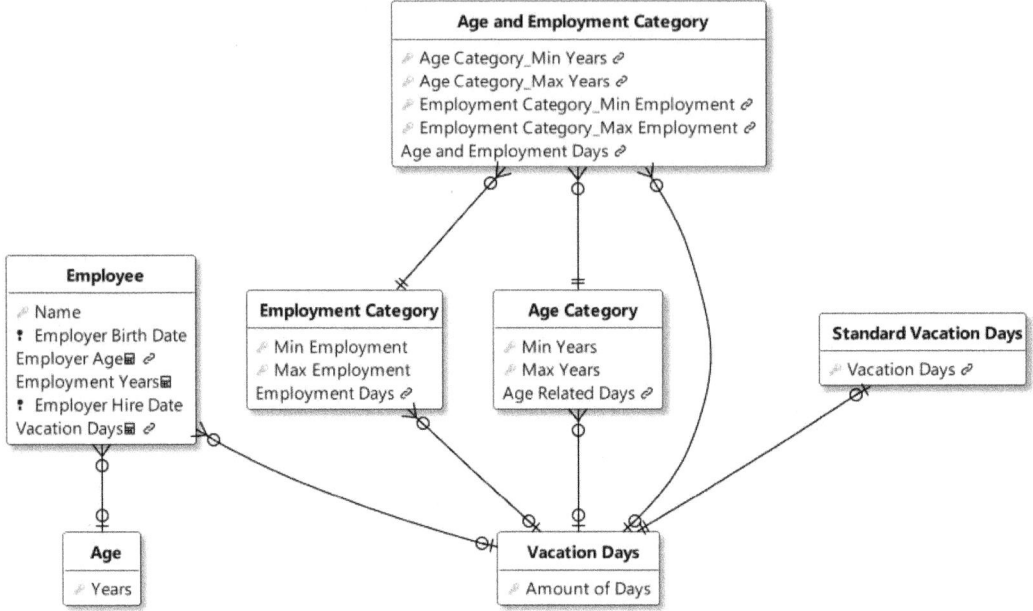

Figure 65: UML from decision table.

13.6 Reference Data Modeling

For more complicated business domains, facts may cover different domains that are still linked. For instance, managing reference data is such a complex architectural domain.

The following diagram shows how Operational Systems contain facts about Country. There exists an external ISO source with two character country codes and their short name and English name. These two need to be linked to provide a standardization for countries used in the company. We provide a fact type called "Country = ISO Country" to link the internal data with the reference data.

Finally, the reference data architecture needs to approve the ISO standard and provide facts on which ISO standard, its status in the organization, and how often we update this external reference data. This diagram demonstrates the power of verbalization and how it integrates multiple domains across architectures.

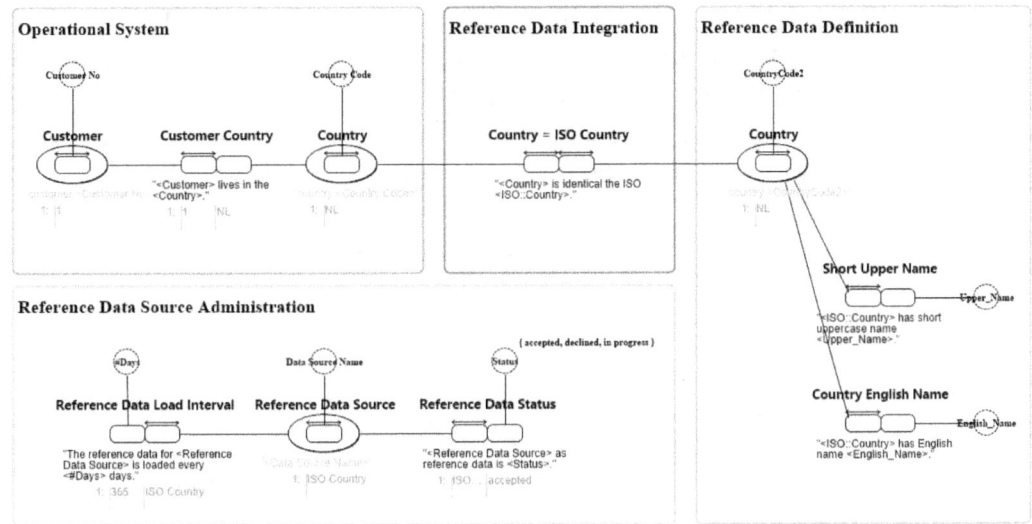

Figure 66: Reference data and metadata modeling.

13.7 Model Annotations

13.7.1 Transitional

Facts can be deceivingly simple until they are registered in different domains or systems at the same time. Lars Rönback explains this beautifully in his presentations and writings.

A simple example is where I could talk about my relationship with my wife and say we are in love. Whereas my wife, after having an argument, states that we are not. This can also happen with data when it needs to be integrated from various sources into a single data warehouse.

Therefore, it is important to register the sources from which these facts are gathered. A simple annotation on the Object or Fact Type may indicate this being in play. System design needs to incorporate this requirement. The diagram below shows there are apparently different sources for appointments, and they may contradict or complement each other regarding appointments made.

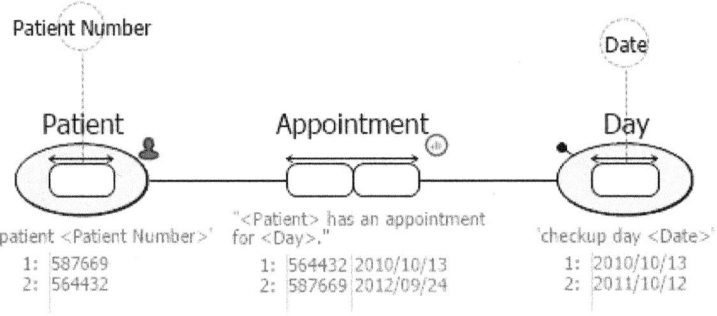

Figure 67: Transitional fact.

13.7.2 Temporal

There are only three business timelines in any business information system. And they may be combined, but it makes asking questions around temporal aspects very simple:

- When is a fact decided?
- When is the fact registered?
- When is the fact valid?

In addition to those three basic business timelines, many more technical may arise. Usually, these must be registered while data is copied from one system to the next. Every transition may need its own timeline.

A simple icon may indicate there are temporal aspects in play.

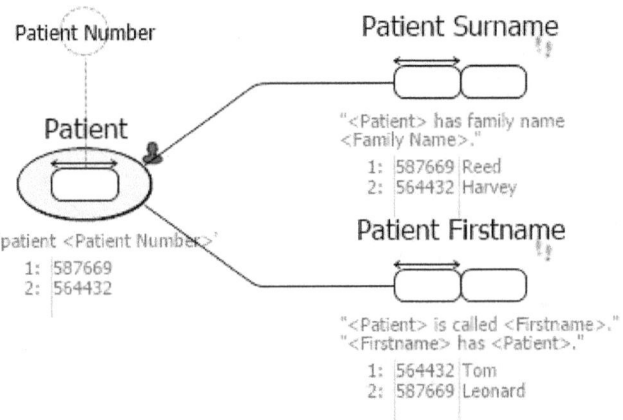

Figure 68: Temporal fact.

Regarding database script generation, CaseTalk will automatically include the required columns to manage the multitude of timelines, enabling temporal in your production system.

13.7.3 Multi-lingual

When entering the multi-lingual world, we need to provide additional storage and structures for translations. A simple annotation in the information model is enough to instruct system developers to add additional measures to facilitate it. For instance, the names of the days of the week may be presented differently in different languages. Therefore, the Weekday Name is annotated.

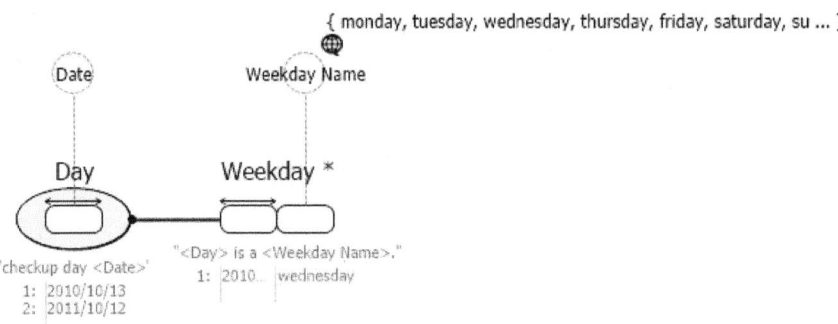

Figure 69: Multi-lingual data.

Additionally, Facts themselves may be entered in multiple languages and need dictionaries for Object and Fact name translations. Once provided with information, models can be depicted in any language with the press of a button. We can also translate all generated technical artifacts by providing technical translations with the information model itself. Below is the exact same information model depicted in Spanish:

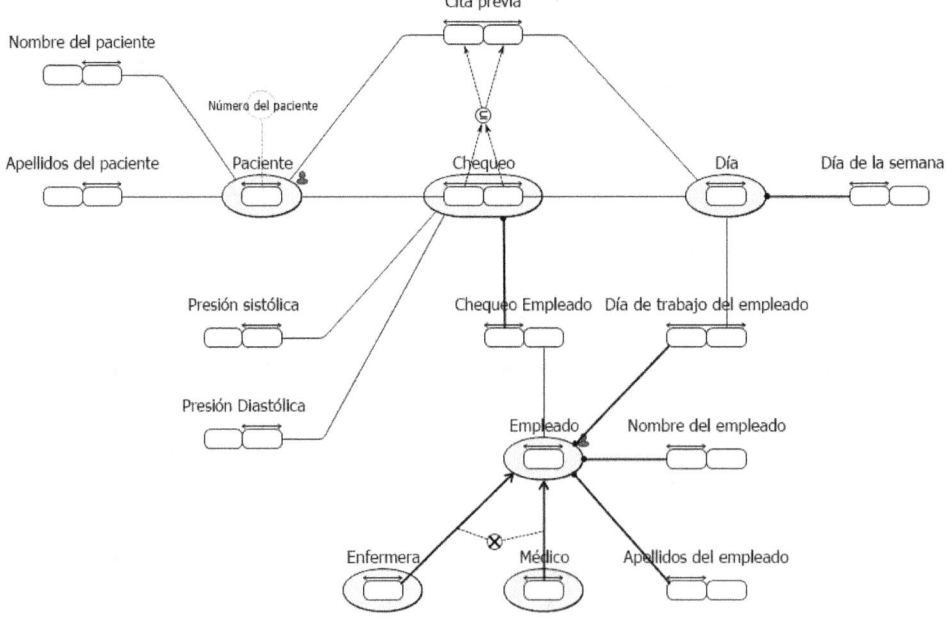

Figure 70: Multi lingual information model.

13.8 PlantUML

PlantUML is an open-source library to generate diagrams of all sorts. It is used in this book and by CaseTalk to create all Logical and UML Class Diagrams and more. It takes simple scripting to define the elements to be drawn. The script to generate Figure 2: Graphical breakdown of a fact expression.

```
@startuml
allow_mixing

' Fact Expression Breakdown

package "Language" as g {
  label " **City of Residence:** \n John Smith lives in The Ne
  therlands." as f
  label " **Country:** \n'The Netherlands' " as country

  label " **Citizen:** \n 'John Smith' " as pers
  }
  note "Fact Expression" as cor
  cor .. f

package "Data" as data {
  label " **Country Name:**\n The Netherlands " as cn

  label " **Firstname:**\n John " as fn
  label " **Surname:**\n Smith " as sn
  }
  country -down- cn
  pers -down- fn
  pers -down- sn
  note "Object Expressions" as note_person
  note_person .. country
  note "Label Types" as note_labels
  note_labels .. cn
  f -down- pers
```

```
    f -down- country

' Bonus: Related Logical Diagram

Object "**Citizen**" as Citizen {

  <&key> FirstName: string
  <&key> Surname: string
  <&badge> Country: string <&link-intact>
  --Semantic--
  **FirstName Surname** lives in **Country**.
  --Example--
  **John Smith** lives in **The Netherlands**.
  }

Object "<&globe> **Country**" as Country {
  <&key> Country Name: string
  --Example--
  **The Netherlands**
  }

Citizen }o--|{ Country : lives in
@enduml
```

Another script which is used to render Figure 70.

```
@startuml
  'note "abc" as abc
  (*) --> if "Patient makes Appointment" then
      -->[true] "Patient shows for Checkup"
    if "Employee is Available" then
      -->[true] "Perform Checkup" as a3
      a3 --> "Register:\n** ** Diastolic Pressure**\n** **
      Systolic Pressure**" as reg
      note right: Determine Blood Pressure Category.
    else
      -->[false] "Reschedule Appointment" as a4
    endif
```

```
    else
        -->[false] "Nothing"
    endif
    reg --> if "Abnormal Result" then
        -->[true] "Make Follow up Appointment" as a5
    else
        -->[false] "No follow up needed"
    endif
@enduml
```

References

Books

Data and Reality: A Timeless Perspective on Perceiving and Managing Information in Our Imprecise World, 3rd Edition, by William Kent. Published by Technics Publications, ISBN 9781935504214.

Fact Oriented Modeling with FCO-IM: Capturing Business Semantics in Data Models with Fully Communication Oriented Information Modeling, by Jan Pieter Zwart, Marco Engelbart, Stijn Hoppenbrouwers. Published by Technics Publications, ISBN 9781634620864.

Invisible Women: Data Bias in a World Designed for Men, by Caroline Criado Pérez. Published by Abrams Press, ISBN 1419729071.

The Culture Map: Breaking Through the Invisible Boundaries of Global Business, by Erin Meyer. Published by Hachette Book Group, ISBN 9781610392501.

The Handbook of Technical Writing, by Gerald J. Alred. Published by St Martins Pr, ISBN 9780312057336.

CaseTalk

The tool used in this book is a case tool called CaseTalk. In early 2002, BCP Software took over maintenance, development, and theoretical research. To this day, it is used by schools, universities, freelancers, and enterprises across the globe.

Since early 2000, insights and feature requests have changed the tool in many ways. Yet, it never lost its focus on being open and true to its origin. All models are open and free to export and import, and licenses for non-profit public schools are available for free.

You may download a free Book Edition from www.casetalk.com.

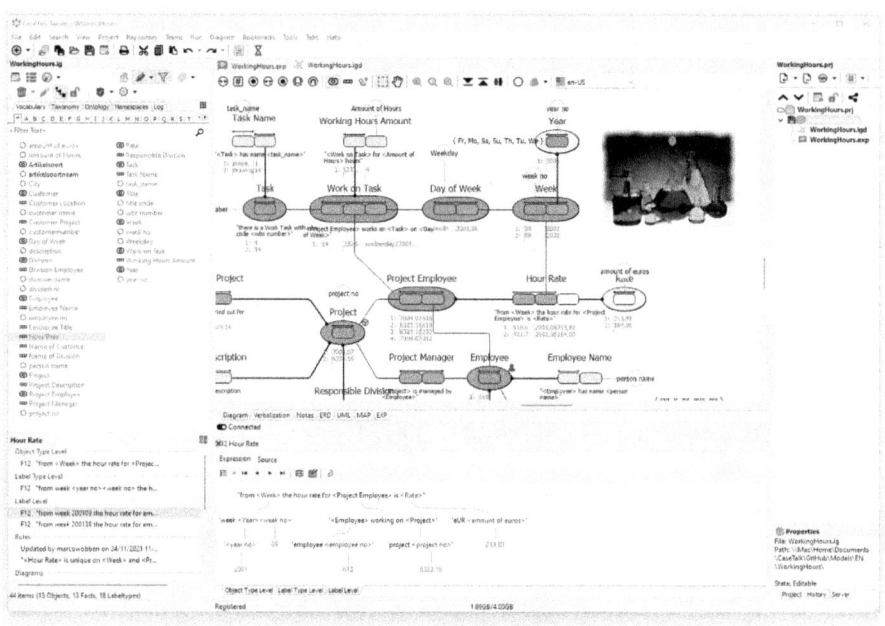

Figure 71: CaseTalk screenprint.

CaseTalk	www.casetalk.com
More Examples	github.com/casetalk
Documentation	www.casetalk.com/wiki
History	time.graphics/line/114267
PlantUML	www.plantuml.com

Methods

FCO-IM	www.fco-im.nl
Wiki	en.wikipedia.org/wiki/Object%E2%80%93role_modeling
Ensemble Logical Modeling	https://www.elmstandards.com/

Experts

Temporal	www.tedamoh.com/en
Transitional	www.linkedin.com/in/ronnback

Index

4GL, 16
abstraction, 41, 42, 81
accountability, 19
Activity Diagram, 97
Agile, 16, 34
AI. See Artificial Intelligence
Anchor Modeling, 108
annotation, 54, 76, 79, 91, 94, 112
architect, 14
architecture, 1, 17, 18, 19, 137
Artificial Intelligence, 16, 124
atomic, 58, 59, 60
Bakema, Guido, 40
BCP Software, 24, 145
big data, 16
business analyst, 14
business information, 8, 10, 13, 15, 17, 22, 23, 32, 37, 40, 41, 47, 48, 51, 64, 100, 138
business needs, 8, 14, 34, 88, 95, 112
CaseTalk, 1, 24, 25, 40, 43, 79, 84, 103, 105, 111, 112, 113, 114, 117, 119, 120, 121, 122, 123, 124, 139, 141, 145, 146
checkups, 45, 46, 55, 72, 126
column store, 105
communication, 7, 8, 11, 21, 24, 27, 29, 30, 31, 39, 42, 45, 54, 55, 57, 63, 75, 76, 82, 87, 88, 92, 94, 104, 112, 117

concept map, 85
concrete, 29, 31, 32, 40, 42, 58, 59, 60, 62, 63, 87, 95, 129
constraint, 43, 54, 65, 66, 67, 68, 69, 70, 71, 74, 76, 79, 84, 95, 96, 103, 106, 107, 109, 114
context, 8, 9, 10, 13, 17, 20, 21, 22, 31, 32, 34, 39, 42, 52, 54, 55, 56, 62, 64, 68, 70, 85, 90, 91, 96
Control Data Corporation Research Laboratory, 24
data
    information vs, 9–10
    origin of, 9
data bias, 19, 34
data contract, 16
Data Definition Language, 114
data event, 16, 98, 117
data governance, 23, 113, 114
data lake, 15
Data Manipulation Language, 114
data mesh, 16
data model, 22, 25, 79, 85
data modeler, 8, 14, 101
data pipeline, 16
data point, 9, 19
data quality, 19, 23, 34, 49
data source, 30, 114
data specialist, 18

data typing, 81
Data Vault, 25, 108, 109
Data Vault Builder, 25
data vs information, 9–10
data warehousing, 15
database, 15, 48, 69, 70, 77, 79, 98, 105, 114, 115, 116, 123, 124, 130, 139
data-driven, 17, 19, 34, 92, 120
data-mesh, 15
DBMS, 114, 115
DDL. See Data Definition Language
decision-making, 9, 19, 20, 22, 34, 91, 114
developer, 1, 14, 18, 47, 50, 74, 116, 121, 132, 139
diagram, 25, 39, 40, 42, 75, 76, 79, 81, 82, 84, 85, 88, 89, 94, 141
digital, 7, 8, 13, 14, 17, 120
DML. See Data Manipulation Language
Domain Driven Design, 121
domain expert, 7, 14, 20, 27, 30, 31, 32, 34, 39, 41, 42, 43, 45, 53, 56, 59, 74, 116, 120, 124, 127
Domain Specific Languages, 121
EAV. See Entity-Attribute-Value
engineer, 8, 18, 101
Ensemble Logical Model, 108
Entity-Attribute-Value, 47
ER/Studio, 25, 124
Event Storming, 121
Excel, 16
fact, 8, 9, 23, 29, 32, 33, 40, 43, 45, 51, 52, 53, 54, 55, 57, 58, 59, 60, 61, 67, 73, 79, 85, 89, 95, 96, 97, 107, 111, 116, 129, 130, 132, 134, 135, 136, 137, 138
fact-oriented information modeling, 39, 79

fact-oriented modeling, 33, 34, 39, 43, 79, 83, 95, 97
Falkenberg, Eckhard, 24
FCO-IM. See Fully Communication Oriented Information Modeling
Focal Point, 108
FOM. See fact-oriented modeling
from data to wisdom, 10
Fully Communication Oriented Information Modeling, 24, 25, 40, 42, 75, 76, 77, 127, 129, 147
functional designer, 14
GDPR, 16
governance, 16, 18, 23, 92, 113, 114
graph, 49
Halpin, Terry, 24
historization, 15
homonym, 42
hub, 109
IBM Systems Journal, 24
information
  business, 10
  data vs, 9–10
information model, 1, 11, 17, 20, 22, 29, 30, 31, 32, 34, 42, 43, 54, 56, 58, 61, 71, 75, 76, 79, 84, 87, 88, 90, 91, 92, 95, 96, 97, 104, 105, 106, 107, 108, 109, 111, 112, 113, 114, 115, 120, 121, 132, 135, 139, 140
information vs data, 9–10
integration, 17, 20, 23, 94, 97, 113
ISO standard, 137
JSON, 45, 117, 119
lexicalization, 105
lexicalize, 103, 104
management, 14, 17, 18, 19, 30, 33, 97, 105, 114, 123
measurement, 100
Meersman, Robert, 24

metadata, 8, 22, 47, 113, 114
metadata management, 22
methodology, 16
microservices, 16
MS-Access, 16
MySQL, 114
N Rule, 66
natural language, 8, 29, 34, 42, 43, 61, 87, 122
Natural language Information Analysis Methodology, 24
Natural Language Processing, 122
NIAM. See Natural language Information Analysis Methodology
Nijssen, G.M., 24
NoSQL, 47, 50
object, 32, 53, 55, 56, 58, 79
object expression, 32
object type, 54
Oracle, 114
origin of data, 9
ORM, 24
OWL. See Web Ontology Language
pattern, 108
physical data model, 77
PlantUML, 141, 146
PostgreSQL, 114
PowerDesigner, 25, 124
process modeler, 14
reduce, 103, 104

relational modeling, 77, 79
Santayana, George, 13
satellite, 109
schema, 79, 117, 118, 119
security, 17, 23
Semantic Web, 120
semantics, 21, 22, 23, 34, 55, 60, 79, 82
Senko, Michael, 23
software development, 14, 16, 81, 121
SQL, 47, 50, 114, 115
SQL Server, 114
stakeholder, 1, 21, 30, 33, 42, 51, 62, 79, 82, 88, 91, 92, 95, 112
Stone Age, 13
strategic, 17
subtype, 73
synonym, 42
taxonomy, 89, 90
technical designer, 14
UML, 25, 76, 81, 82, 83, 84, 105, 132, 141
Universe of Discourse, 29
unstructured, 15
value, 29, 32, 53, 54, 55, 56, 58, 60, 63, 69, 72, 84, 89
van der Lek, Harm, 1, 40, 58
vertical architecture, 19
Web Ontology Language, 120
XML, 45, 117, 119
Zwart, JanPieter, 1, 40

www.ingramcontent.com/pod-product-compliance
Lightning Source LLC
LaVergne TN
LVHW081528060526
838200LV00045B/2034